IDENTITY THEFT

IDENTITY
THEFT

reclaiming your freedom in Christ

Ken White

Whitecaps Media
Houston, Texas
www.whitecapsmedia.com

Identity Theft: Reclaiming Your Freedom in Christ
© 2010 Ken White
All rights reserved
ISBN: 978-0-9826353-3-9

Printed in the United States of America

To the memory of
Matthew Ryan Beveridge
1988–2008

CONTENTS

NOTE TO THE READER

The concepts in this book have been written about from many different perspectives over many decades, but almost always in a dull and scholarly way.

However, as you will see, this book is far from dull! My hope is that reading it will stimulate great conversations between you and God and others about a notion that we are just not that aware of. Finally, my prayer is that you are closer to Jesus when you finish reading what is between these covers.

FORE!

Novice. Rookie. Greenhorn. Beginner. All of those terms apply to me when it comes to golf. I'm not a golfer. I am a world-class hacker, which is, however, much more entertaining on the golf course. Give me a five iron, a putter and maybe a wedge and I'm good to go. My sparse club selection only reinforces my novice status, along with how many times I have found myself shouting down range "FORE!"

For those of you who may be less familiar with golf and its corresponding lingo, "FORE!" is what you yell at the top of your lungs after you have hit an errant shot that threatens bodily harm to someone somewhere on the golf course. Ideally, innocent bystanders will hear your desperate plea for their attention and run for cover.

In many ways I feel that I have teed it up, waggled, and let it fly with this book. So as fair warning:

FORE!

Not that I think anything in this book is out of bounds. Quite the contrary. I believe it is right down the middle of the fairway.

My prayer, however, is that somewhere at some point you will have to run for cover. I hope that something you read; some verse, some quote, some thought that pops into your head, will move you. I mean quite literally move you.

This is not a book that will encourage you to find yourself, become a better you, or help you win friends and influence people. For quite some time, Christians have struggled with a faith experience that has been dutiful at best, dry and unfulfilling at worst. We have fallen victim to a spiritual identity theft. In cases of financial identity theft, victims live for a period of time completely unaware that someone is actively spending their money, wrecking their credit, and trashing their reputation. As Christians, we are completely unaware that our identity as ones who are beloved, free, approved of, pursued, and desired beyond our wildest dreams has been shrouded at best and stolen at worst.

What this book will do is help you recover your identity as a redeemed child of God and then convince you to move out into the grace, fulfillment, and freedom that intimacy with God—and only intimacy with God—brings.

I didn't really learn to read—that is, really read—until I was in seminary. That might sound odd, but it's true. One of my professors would pick up a book off a student's desk and taunt it: "What are you going to teach me? What do you know that I don't?" I haven't picked up a book since without engaging in a little taunting myself.

I hope you will do the same with this book. Grab hold of it and demand, "What am I going to get out of you!? What are you going to tell me that I don't already know!?"

Don't be surprised, though, if it does some taunting of its own and calls you to the most exciting adventure known to man—living your life in total dependence and deep intimacy with Jesus Christ.

Grace and Peace.

—KEN WHITE
Corpus Christi, Texas
October 2010

1

SANDBOATS

Years ago I heard a story about fleas. It went something like this: Get some fleas. Put the fleas in a jar. Poke holes in the lid and screw the lid on the jar. Watch the fleas jump around in the jar. You'll notice that they will jump all over the jar. They will even bounce right off the lid of the jar. Wait for a couple of days and then remove the lid.

You would think it would be a jailbreak for the little guys. The way the story goes, though, the fleas do not jump out after the lid is removed because they learned earlier they cannot jump out, now they don't even try.

After a little online cruising, I found that the story came from Zig Ziglar's book, *See You at the Top*. Evidently, within the thriving flea circus industry, a need exists to train fleas to stay in one place for extended periods of time. Can't say I've ever seen a flea circus. Nevertheless this all must be accurate because, as many a high school student has said, "Dude, it's true. I Googled it."

During my online excursion I also learned some fun facts to know and tell about fleas, like:

- The largest recorded flea is the North American

Hystrichopsylla schefferi, measuring twelve milli-meters in length—almost ½-inch!

- The female flea consumes fifteen times her own body weight in blood daily.

- Some fleas can jump 150 times their own length. That compares to a human jumping 1,000 feet. One flea broke a record with a four-foot vertical jump.[1]

If you Google "fleas, jar" you will find approximately 116,000 web pages that will tell you the "fleas in a jar" story in its various forms. You will also learn there are about 116,000 multi-level marketers who are pretty sure you are not living up to your full potential in life. About twelve web pages into my online foray, my skepti-cism about Pavlovian fleas began to be whipped into a frenzy. In an attempt to soothe my aching doubt, I de-cided to put the story to the test. OK, in reality, my kids were bored one summer morning and since I'd always wanted to know about the fleas …

The family dogs met the experiment with mixed emo-tions. Bessie Belle, the bulldog-boxer mix, is a sucker for any kind of attention. It didn't matter that the kids were pulling tufts of hair off of her in the full-body gropefest. She was in heaven. Buster, the fox-bird-snake-squirrel-rat-possum terrier was much less impressed.

The first realization came after about three months of searching for our fleas: Flea prevention technology has obviously progressed exponentially from where it was when I was a kid. Back in the day, we had the flim-sy white flea collar that supposedly killed the fleas on contact as they made their way to water themselves at the dog's nose.

Let's get past the fact that this explanation never sat well with me either.

With our current flea and tick regimen it took us two months to find two fleas. Two months! Who knew?

We finally get our two fleas in a jar. Sure enough, just like the story said, there they were jumping around like crazy. Also, just like the story said, they bounced off the inside of the lid over and over and over again.

After a couple of days we took the lid off the jar. Sure enough those fleas absolutely did not jump out of that jar. The explanation quickly became apparent for why fleas don't jump out of the jar when the lid is removed.

They're dead.

OK, if they're not dead they have beaten themselves into a vegetative state. When the lid came off, one of the unlucky participants was DOA. The other one was making eerie spastic jerking movements, which traumatized the seven- and ten-year-old children.

All in all, we're going to say the fleas-in-a-jar experiment was not a success.

I'm not saying fleas can't learn to stay in a confined space. I'm just saying it sure looked like our two fleas beat themselves to death trying to get out of their little prison.

Our fleas-in-a-jar experiment was a little disappointing. There was a part of me that wanted to see the process work. It didn't. It did, however, put some things into perspective for me. It made me think about my life. It made me think about how, for many years of my life, I felt like I was beating myself to death against an invisible ceiling. One day, as I reflected on those years of my life, I was driving down Ocean Drive in Corpus Christi, Texas, watching the sailboats out on the bay. Seeing the sailboats glide effortlessly through the water seemed to jostle this memory loose. Memories are shadowy at first, but as this one became clear in my mind, I began to see how it could help illustrate this problem of identity theft.

My friend Jack was on a business trip. He finished his presentation early and had some time before he had to get to the airport. Since he was in a beach town, he thought he would head over and enjoy the seashore for a while.

He was only at the beach a few minutes before he noticed a sailboat out in the distance. It caught his attention because it just stayed in one spot. It was in the ocean but it wasn't sailing. It quickly became obvious that the sailboat had become stuck on a sandbar as the tide receded.

Jack could tell there was a family in the boat and it seemed like the father needed help. So Jack rolled up the pant legs of his suit and waded out to see if he could help. After a couple of hours of digging and pushing and pulling, the sailboat was out of the sand and back into the ocean where it belonged—gliding freely through the water.

When Jack told this story, he was simply relaying this really odd thing that happened to him on his last business trip. The story was full of strange twists and turns that mostly centered on how foolish Jack was feeling while he was digging a boat out of the sand in a business suit while the children clambered around the boat without a care in the world. I, however, was captivated by the image of this sailboat stuck in the sand. To me it painted such a clear picture of our lives.

That sailboat was created. It was built piece by piece by a master builder. In his mind's eye, the builder could see this sailboat before it was even finished. He knew what color he was going to paint it. He knew how it would sit in the water. He knew how it would lean over in a heavy wind. The master builder intended every part that he crafted to fit together into a beautiful, sleek sailboat that would slide effortlessly through the waves.

Yet at the time Jack saw this boat it was beached; run aground amidst the very ocean it was intended to master with grace and elegance. Stuck in the sand it was nothing more than a glorified, intimately crafted playground attraction. Stuck in the sand the sailboat was no longer a sailboat. It was a sandboat. And as long as it sat in the sand, it was never going to fulfill the purpose it was so carefully crafted for.

Like the sailboat, intimately crafted in the master builder's workshop, you and I have been knit together in our mother's womb. We have been designed and built by a Master Craftsman. You existed in the mind of God before you became the masterpiece you are now. You are the tangible manifestation of the intangible thoughts of God. You are the visible expression of the love of God.

"Long before he laid down earth's foundations, God had us in mind, had settled on us as the focus of his love, to be made whole and holy by his love."[2]

He made every part of you with the specific intent that you spend your days gliding through the waters of life. Unfortunately, though, many of us are like that sailboat. We are stuck.

Graciously, because it is made of wood and canvas, a sailboat has no idea it is stuck. It cannot grasp the tragedy of its predicament. As cognitive human beings, though, many of us sit stuck in the sand fully aware of our reality.

I don't know about you but there have been times in my life when I have felt like a colossal, world class, Olympic size *sandboat*. I've also spent twenty years in ministry looking into the bewildered eyes of a humanity that looks longingly to the sea for answers the sea will never give them. Life may be the ocean that you were meant to sail through, but life itself is never going to give you the answers you need. We are stuck because we have been robbed. Our very identity has come into question. We have been told we are *sandboats* when we know full well we are *sailboats*.

2

BITTERSWEET
SYMPHONY

*'Cause it's a bittersweet symphony this life. Trying to
make ends meet you're a slave to money then you die.*

—THE VERVE

"BITTERSWEET SYMPHONY"

*There is no theory of evolution. Just a list of animals
Chuck Norris allows to live.*

—CHUCKNORRISFACTS.COM

*Freedom: A state of living without being subject to
restraint.*

—WEBSTER'S DICTIONARY

Back in the sixties things were different. I don't mean
Haight-Ashbury, Woodstock, or any of the other iconic
places or events that defined that era. I'm talking about the
zoo. As the sixties turned to the seventies, I was only six so
I don't remember much. But I do remember the zoo.

I remember going to the Houston Zoo when I was
a kid. The lions and tigers and primates were in, well

there's really no other way to say it: they were in jail. I remember walking along this long row of large cages. Each cage contained a different species of monkey. I have this distinct memory of passing by each cage looking at the monkeys as they would look back at me. I thought it was odd, but at six years old I had no idea why I thought it was odd. As I look back at it now, it was not that I felt sorry for the monkeys because they were in cages. I felt sorry for them because the cages were so sterile—nothing but steel bars and concrete floors.

Nowadays it's different. Zoos have invested big money in "exotic habitats." The habitats are large and authentically landscaped. The last time I visited a zoo, I'm not sure I actually ever saw an animal. That makes me feel much better for the animals but because they blend in so well in such a large environment, they are almost impossible to see.

This is definitely not a plug for PETA or The Humane Society. It is interesting to note, though, that we have moved from small, sterile cages to large, authentic habidomes as a means of displaying wildlife. It seems, at some level, we have recognized that to confine a wild animal to a sterile cage is to diminish it.

A majestic lion in a sterile cage is akin to a beautiful sailboat stuck on a sandbar. Concrete and steel have a way of draining the ferocious majesty right out of the king of beasts.

To come face to face with a 500-pound lion when it is behind two inches of bullet-proof safety glass is one thing. To come face to face with a 500-pound lion in the

African savannah is a completely different experience. I once saw a video on YouTube that showed this in vivid detail.

This video began with a large male lion pacing in the distance, partially obscured by tall savannah grasses. As he turns broadside to the camera, a shot rings out and the lion drops from view. A second later his head pops up above the tall grass. Watching the video I had the sense the lion is thinking to himself, *What the heck just happened?*

The video cuts to a group of hunters running to the right of the screen. They pull up and begin to fire. It takes a second to figure out what is happening. The *massive* lion is charging the hunters, dust popping up from the ground around it as they continue to fire at it. As it approaches the group at full speed it rears back on its hind legs to attack one of the hunters. Instantaneously another hunter has crouched to one knee and gets off an extremely lucky shot, knocking the lion off balance. The lion flies by its intended mark and rolls violently in the dust—but not before it got a piece of one of the hunters. The segment ends with the lion fleeing as the hunters continue to fire at it.

I was captivated by this video because it pitted one lion against five people, five people with some of the biggest guns on the face of the planet. Twelve seconds and seven rifle shots into the chaotic scene, the lion is still alive, has almost ripped one person to shreds and one set of incredibly lucky hunters are fortunate they did not shoot one or more of their own hunting party.

The hunters in this video learned in life-flashing-before-your-eyes fashion why lions are called apex predators.

Chuck Norris or not, one-on-one in the wilderness, a lion will own you. To me, a lion in a cage brings a sadness to my heart for the simple reason that its identity as a ferociously beautiful creation has been diminished.

Diminishing the identity of a flea, a sailboat, a monkey, or a lion is one thing. Diminishing the identity of a human being is on a completely different moral plane. Some of the great atrocities in the world have occurred after one group of people has diminished the identity of another group of people. Serbia, Rwanda, Cambodia, and Nazi Germany are only a few recent examples of what happens when people are reduced to something other than human. The atrocities themselves are reprehensible, but a greater evil was first committed when the identity of others was diminished. Italian Holocaust survivor Primo Levi wrote,

> Before dying the victim must be degraded so that
> the murderer will be less burdened by guilt. This
> is an explanation not devoid of logic but it shouts
> to heaven; it is the sole use of useless violence.[1]

Degrading, devaluing, or diminishing the identity of a human being is evil. It is an evil that reaches the ears of God and pierces his very heart.

Like a lion in a sterile cage, part of our humanity—our human identity—is based on freedom. Like a sailboat's ability to glide effortlessly through the water and like a lion's ability to roam uncontested through the wild, mankind has been given a gift of matchless value. It is the gift of free will. It is a gift unique among all living creatures. It is the essence of the human identity.

The words "free will" cannot be spoken without some idea of what "free" means. Webster's defines "freedom" as the "total absence of restraint." Most people would agree with that definition not just in principle but also in practice. Our lives seem to bear that out. In many ways life seems to be less about the pursuit of *happiness* and more about the pursuit of *less restraint*.

Less time at work.

Less time driving to work.

Less time away from the family.

Less time making money (more time spending it!).

Less time doing what others want.

Less time doing what I have to do.

Humanity's romance with this kind of freedom has blinded us to this truth: True freedom has nothing to do with a lack of restraint. This blindness has diminished us and this is not the only way our human dignity is degraded when we throw off restraint in pursuit of what we want.

A young girl's virginity is taken.

A father communicates to his son that he is worthless and will never amount to anything.

A prisoner of war is humiliated.

A husband tells his wife he is leaving.

An employer takes advantage of an employee.

A mother tells her daughter she should dress

differently so the boys will like her. All of the above have diminished someone's identity as someone else—a parent, boss, boyfriend—pursued their own "freedom."

I am pure. I am valuable. I am desired. I am the object of affection. I am safe. I am whole. I am confident. I am free. When these things are taken from someone, it is more than wrong, unfortunate, or counter-productive. Diminishing the God-given identity of another is an act of violence against the soul, against God himself.

It is evil.

Whether we want to admit it or not, we have suffered much the same fate as the fleas in the jar. Our identity has been diminished when we believe the definition of "freedom" as simply the lack of restraint. Our identity has been diminished when we do not engage our free will for the simple purpose of experiencing freedom. What if our definition of freedom has kept us from understanding true freedom? What if the reality of freedom is far greater than a mere lack of restraint?

We are a culture that is built upon individual liberty and freedom: freedom to assemble, freedom to bear arms, and freedom of the press. Could it be that in our almost neurotic preoccupation with freedom that we have completely missed what individual freedom really is? At least what it means to be truly free?

Our view of freedom is skewed because we have made a basic error in how we define freedom. We have made the faulty assumption that freedom is an end in itself. Because we have made this assumption, freedom is something we pursue as a destination, as a goal, as a place we will arrive at. As we will see, however, true freedom is not an end in itself. As lofty as our ideals of freedom are, true freedom is of a completely different nature.

Our view of freedom is jaded because our identity has been compromised, assaulted, and in some cases straight-up stolen. That's OK, though. We're in good company.

3
THE HEART OF THE MATTER

If you are the Son of God, tell these stones to become bread.

—MATTHEW 4:3

MMMMMiss It, Noonan...

—CADDYSHACK

There is a great, although highly underrated competition in American youth culture. It is a game where hand-eye coordination is developed, creativity is demanded, and the art of the taunt is honed to perfection. There may be no other activity that brings together such varied demands on a young soul. Since the inception of basketball, many a junior high boy has gained mad basketball skills while locked in a viciously competitive game of .... H-O-R-S-E.

The usual human thing to do when faced with the task of completely discouraging an opponent is to question his or her *ability*.

I know this.

Many games of H-O-R-S-E in my driveway came down to the last shot. It's H-O-R-S to H-O-R-S. Pete Johnson lines up the infamous backwards-granny-free-throw shot. It's a low percentage, last ditch attempt to take me at the buzzer. Pete positions himself to shoot: the awkward, extreme arching of the back to find the now upside-down goal on the roof of the garage. He spins the basketball between his hands. He dribbles the ball one more time. This was my sign that he was about to make the shot. So, like any self-respecting junior high boy would do, I begin to chant "Mmmmmmmmmiss, it Noonan. Miss it! Mmmmmmmmmmiss it. You're gonna mmmmmiss it, Noonan! Miss it!" (We lifted this taunt from the movie, *Caddyshack*). This was a 1980s, northwest Houston suburban version of "Heeeeey badda, badda. Hey badda, badda, SWING!"

Somehow, most of the time, the historically low percentage backwards-granny-free-throw in the hands of Pete Johnson magically became an incredibly high percentage shot when it was for the game. No amount of taunting and distraction seemed to kill the backwards-granny-free-throw shot when it was for the "E."

In the end I did learn from H-O-R-S-E that most human efforts at discouragement focus on questioning the *ability* of your intended target. If you really want to play dirty pool, you can ratchet it up a notch and question someone's character or integrity. Thankfully, though, we usually stick to casting doubt on our opponent's ability.

This is not what happened, though, one day in the

desert two thousand years ago. In this exchange we find evil itself squaring off against God incarnate. As we will see, Satan obviously knew something about Jesus well before the rest of us did.

Before Jesus began his ministry, he was led into the wilderness to be tested. Satan is waiting for him there. Being his supremely prideful and rebellious self, the prince of darkness is the definition of a "player." He believes he can "play" the God-man. If he cannot persuade him to join his cause, he will at least try to trip him up. There is no mystery in the attempt. What is astounding and educational is the method the devil used in the effort.

The very first thing Satan says to Jesus does not call Jesus' ability into question. He swings for the fences and blatantly calls Jesus' *identity* itself into question: "*If you are the Son of God*, tell these stones to become bread."[1] Immediately, Satan goes to the heart of the matter: "IF you are the Son of God ..."

In the epic battle of good versus evil, Satan is not taunting Jesus with the equivalent of "Miss it, Noonan!" He is not saying, "Hey, I know you are God in a man-suit, but this whole 'incarnation' thing is a low percentage, last-ditch attempt at the redemption of man."

Satan is not questioning Jesus' ability. He is not even questioning his integrity. He is questioning his identity.

By saying "*If* you are the Son of God," Satan is simply telling Jesus, "C'mon kid, give it up. You're not the Son of God. You're mistaken. You're just another wannabe rebel with a messiah complex."

31

The Deceiver trying to deceive? Naaah! He doesn't do that!

He does, has, and will continue to deceive. We see it clearly in this passage. We can understand that Jesus was tempted in the wilderness, but somehow we disconnect that from our own journey. We miss a simple fact: If Satan went after Jesus this way, he has and will continue to come at us in the same way.

Satan. Lucifer. The devil. He has many names, but he only has two tools: accusation and deception. But that is closely akin to saying Michelangelo or DaVinci only had two tools: a paintbrush and a chisel. Satan is a technician, an artist with malevolent intent who has had eons to perfect his discipline. The object of his discipline is you.

It is not very "PC" to talk about hate. But to say that you have a supernatural enemy that "really, really dislikes" you just doesn't quite do the job. If it was not for the consistent, pre-existent, intervening grace of God, your enemy would have already squashed your head and pulled off your arms and legs. Does that help put it in perspective?

How Satan feels about us is way past simple hatred. He loathes you. He despises you because you were created in the image of God by God for God. He would love nothing more than to end you for that very reason. The band Nickelback has a song called, "How You Remind Me." A line in the chorus reads, "This is how you remind me of what I really am." You remind the father of lies of what he really is. He is well aware his time is coming.

Misery loves company. He just wants to take you with him when he goes.

Your identity has been assaulted. It has been assaulted by no one less than the devil himself.

And unfortunately he is not the only one that wants a piece of you. There are two other elements that form a sort of triumvirate of evil. In contrast to the Holy Trinity, there is what some have called an "unholy trinity": the enemy (that is, Satan), the world, and the flesh.

When "world" is used in Scripture, it has three basic meanings. The first meaning refers to the earth, as in, "He was in the *world*, and though the *world* was made through him …"[2] The second meaning refers to the inhabitants of the earth, as in, "For God so loved the *world* that he gave his one and only Son, that whoever believes in him shall not perish but have eternal life."[3] Finally, the last meaning of world can be defined loosely as an organized system with an agenda that is set against God. The apostle John uses this sense of the word in First John: "Do not love the *world* or anything in the *world*. If anyone loves the *world*, the love of the Father is not in him."[4]

It is this third definition of "the world" that makes up the second part of the unholy trinity. For reasons we will see in detail in chapter 6, the "world" came out of the Fall of Man. Once sin broke onto the scene, every aspect of our existence became FUBAR'd (Fouled Up Beyond All Recognition).

This is why you might feel like you are living your life in wet cement sometimes. No matter how hard or intense the effort, you feel like you are slogging slowly through life. "The world" is literally working against you. Remember that this designation is a spiritual definition. Scripture is clear:

> For though we live in the world, we do not wage war as the world does. The weapons we fight with are not the weapons of the world. On the contrary, they have divine power to demolish strongholds. We demolish arguments and every pretension that sets itself up against the knowledge of God, and we take captive every thought to make it obedient to Christ.[5]

People are not your enemy. The enemy is your enemy, and the "world" is where the battle takes place.

The last element of the unholy trinity is the flesh. As Christians we can know that our hearts of stone have been replaced with hearts of flesh.[6] We are new creations in Christ.[7] This new birth, however, took place in our old body. This is not a news flash: Your flesh and spirit are at war with one another. This is why you need to know who you are. Are you a helpless victim stuck in a cage awaiting your next drubbing? Are you a sailboat that is just going to have to get used to life on this sandbar?

That is not the way Jesus dealt with the enemy when *his* identity was assaulted.

When his identity was called into question, Jesus' response was beautiful in its simple truth: "Man does not live by bread alone, but by every word that proceeds from God's mouth." Since Satan called his identity into question, it would be worth looking at what has come out of God's mouth about the identity of Jesus Christ.

Here are just a few of the over one hundred names Jesus is called in Scripture: God,[8] Prince of Peace,[9] God with us,[10] Alpha and Omega,[11] Bread of Life,[12] Christ,[13] Creator,[14] Word of God,[15] True Light,[16] Righteous One.[17]

Since our identity has been assaulted, too, it's worth looking at what God says about *us*.

Did you know that God rejoices over you with singing?[18] He catches your tears in a bottle.[19] In Christ, you are the righteousness of God.[20] You are his bride.[21] God's heart turns within him for you. God's heart does backflips when he thinks of you![22]

We must hold fast to the things God says about us. We must listen intently to the father heart of God. We must live by every word that proceeds from the mouth of God. He is not just "fond" of you. God does not just "love" you. (We throw "love" around to the point it becomes cheapened—we "love" a good cheeseburger, for heaven's sake!). God is crazy about you! You were conceived in the mind of a God who creates from love, not need. You have been loved perfectly from that time up to this very instant.

In the face of a relentless message that consistently attempts to devalue you, do what Jesus did: Tell the world, the enemy, and your flesh what God has told you. Do not let the unholy trinity diminish your identity.

4

TALK TO THE HAND

All great things are simple, and many can be expressed in single words: freedom, justice, honor, duty, mercy, hope.

—SIR WINSTON CHURCHILL

Everybody wants me to be what they want me to be. I'm not happy when I try to fake it.

—THE COMMODORES
"EASY"

Living out of the false self creates a compulsive desire to present a perfect image to the public so that everybody will admire us and nobody will know us.

—BRENNAN MANNING

Who told you you were naked?

—GOD

As a college student in the eighties there was one thing that really chapped me. You ready? Here it is: "Yes, Mr. White, that is a good observation, *but don't you think your conclusions are a little too simplistic?*"

Simplistic.

Have you ever been beaten down by that word? We

all know it. What they might as well be saying is, "You stupid, stupid little boy. Do you not know that the workings of the universe are far, far away from the grasp of your tiny little mind?"

In our post-modern, relativistic, deconstructivist world, everything has to be so complicated.

You know what?

I'm with Winston Churchill. Some things are simple. Some of the greatest things about life are simple.

The way my daughter, Mikaela, picks up a bug and holds it up close so she can see every part of it: simple curiosity. The way my children would jump to me from the side of the pool: simple trust. The way I love my wife: it's not complicated; it's simple.

One plus one equals two. That's not complicated. It's simply true. Here's something else that is simple and true, but I sure didn't learn it in college.

We all operate from one of two places in life: being *loved* or being *known*.

I spent the first thirty years of my life operating from a place of trying to be loved. I mean, why not? Being loved is great. We love to be loved. We love to hear, "You da man! You're awesome! I love you! You're the best!" There is nothing wrong with wanting to be loved. We were made to be loved. The problem comes when we don't realize that there is a huge opportunity cost when we operate from the place of being loved. It comes at the cost of being *known*.

The human soul desires more than anything to be known...*and loved*. But we settle for being loved because we don't believe we can be known *and loved.*

Our real motivation for being loved isn't really the warm fuzzies that come from being loved. Our real motivation for settling with just being loved is fear. The mind-bending, soul-killing fear that we cannot be loved *and known.*

Let's face it, in our deep hearts we all believe, "If you really knew me, there is no way in H-E-double-hockey-sticks you could love me. If you only knew what I really thought about. If you only knew what I was doing when nobody is around." Yes, even the "it-takes-more-mus-cles-to-frown-than-to-smile"-type of person can feel this way. Some of the most positive people in the world are also some of the most unknowable.

My friend (and ridiculously-brilliant-scholar-type) Clay Butler had a social studies teacher in middle school who liked to say, "Man's greatest need isn't to be loved, because he is already perfectly loved. What we need is to *know* that we are loved." Clay puts it more simply, "You can go to the beach or you can go to the mountains, but you can't do both at the same time." In doing one, you eliminate the other. There is no difference in deciding whether you will live from being loved or being known. You will, however, have to choose which place you are going to live from.

We all operate from one of these two places. Some have a hard time accepting the loved-or-known concept. Many want to say we operate from both places at the same time. Others believe we need to change the termi-nology to more of an "acceptance/rejection" framework.

Yet others believe the concept is more complex than a simplistic "loved and known" approach.

Obviously, I wouldn't be writing this book if I believed it wasn't as simple as deciding, "Today, I'm going to choose to be known instead of loved." Does that thought make you feel a little uncomfortable? Does that set off a little twinge of apprehension in your gut just thinking about it? If so, you may be working from a place of being loved. But again, I have observed that that is where most of us as broken human beings live.

Since most of us are pretty convinced we cannot be known and loved … we fake it. Brennan Manning puts it like this: *"Living out of the false self creates a compulsive desire to present a perfect image to the public so that everybody will admire us and nobody will know us."* [1]

We fake it because we can hold out to one person one thing and to another person another. Sometimes when I'm speaking in public, I ask people to hold their hands in front of their faces like a mask (you can do this too if you like). It doesn't matter which way. Palm out or palm in. The point is that your hand hides your face. It covers your identity. If someone is standing in front of you looking at your face, they will see a portion of your face but they will mostly see your hand. The hand in front of your face represents the person you want others to accept as the real you.

If you just put your hand in front of your face palm in, change it to palm out. Bam! That was easy. You just "changed" yourself. Who said change wasn't easy? Your wife likes the thoughtful, palm-facing-in version of you, but your boss likes the aggressive, palm-facing-out version of you. Your friends like the palm-facing-in-make-a-fist version of you, and your parents another and someone else another and another …

Is this too simplistic?

I don't think so. This is where the vast majority of humanity lives. Are you faking your way through life because you are convinced you can't move your hand away from your face? Are you tired of the never-ending performance? You don't like this hand? Then I'll make it this. Oh, you don't like that? Then I'll make it this.

This is why we fake it. We believe that, once we are seen in our nakedness with none of our bells and whistles, we will not be loved and we may possibly be rejected.

In *The Beatitudes*, Simon Tugwell observes:

> We either flee our own reality or manufacture a false self which is mostly admirable, mildly prepossessing, and superficially happy. We hide what we know or feel ourselves to be (which we assume to be unacceptable and unlovable) behind some kind of appearance which we hope will be more pleasing. We hide behind pretty faces, which we put on for the benefit of our public. And in time we may even forget that we are hiding, and think that our assumed pretty face is what we really look like.[2]

Hiding is a universal trait. Three of the most devastating words in all of Scripture are, "And they hid."[3] As soon as sin entered the world, we started hiding. Before sin, nakedness was freedom. Sin brought with it a consciousness of good and evil that cast nakedness as vulnerability. Vulnerability brings hiding.

While we hide, though, our inner person cries out, "I am here! I want to be known! I yearn to be known intimately. I am tired of jumping through hoops so that I can experience love. But if you had a clear look at my face, you would know me and you would not love me, and I could not live with that. I don't want to fake it anymore, but I am afraid that if I show you the real me, you will walk away. I can't handle that kind of pain, so I will go on pretending. I can't even handle the thought of that kind of pain, so I will stuff every thought of being known into the corners of my soul."

The basic assumption in all of this is: "Who I really am is not good enough." The basic lie in all of this is: "Who I really am is not good enough."

It's tragic, but we truly believe we can change a particular image we want people to see, but we can't change ourselves. Who told us that being us in all of our nakedness was bad? Who told us that what God created wasn't good enough?

It sure wasn't God.

God "looked at everything he had made and saw that it was *excellent in every way.*"[4] He is not up in heaven right now shouting down, "Look at everything I have made! It is awesome! Well, it's awesome except for you. Yeah, you, buddy. You right there reading the book. Everything is excellent except for *you*! You happen to be really messed up and beyond repair."

God has not singled you out for non-excellent status. He really hasn't.

That face that looks back at you from the mirror represents the real you. As soon as you raise that hand to obscure your God-given identity, you have bought in to the lie that you alone just aren't good enough.

God created us but we didn't like what we saw so we put our hands to our faces. We have obscured our identity. Intentionally or unintentionally is not the issue. This is our reality. Do we really think that what God made is so inadequate that we have to add on, augment, or otherwise improve the creation of the living God of the Universe?

We have been robbed. When we believe that what God intended is inadequate, we have been ripped off. A colossal act of identity theft was perpetrated on mankind when we decided to fake it. Our identity as perfect sailboats created to bring glory to God is diminished when we believe anything contrary to what God says about us.

We have exchanged God's truth about us for the lie that we are nothing but useless sandboats run aground in the sea that is life.

Christians and non-Christians alike are adept at faking it because the condition is universal across humanity. We have elevated faking it to an art form. Other than being driven by a neurotic fear of being "found out," we fake it because our alter egos are pliable and flexible. We have learned from infancy that we can change how others perceive us by making alterations to the hand in

43

front of our faces. Our successes and failures at tweaking our alter egos have hard-wired this behavior into our daily lives.

We do this not just because it is how we have learned to live life, but because we are convinced we can't change who we really are. We have been persuaded by the gnawing doubt that, "If I move my hand from my face, that will only leave me, and I know I can't change myself."

That is absolutely correct. You can't change yourself! But praise be to God, he will, can, and is able to do more than you could ask or imagine.[5] He decided long before you were born that you would change.[6] He already knows what you will look like as these changes occur: Jesus.

I need to warn you. You may experience a strange new sensation when you decide to be known and loved instead of only loved. It may do things like make you feel like you can speak your mind. You might begin to think that your opinions are actually worth talking about. This feeling may make you want to run through the grass barefoot. You may begin to feel in your deep heart that you really are a sailboat and take your life out to the open sea. You may begin to sense something you haven't felt since childhood. It won't take you long to recognize this new sensation, though. It's freedom. Blessed, made-in-heaven, God-ordained freedom.

This kind of freedom is not just the mere lack of restraint. This is a freedom of the soul. It is a freedom that launches dreams and visions. It's a freedom no one can take from you. It can't be taken because it is not contingent on some outside force. Being known is simply an act of your will.

Remember the caged lion and the imprisoned fleas? Settling for pseudo-love when our hearts' desire is to be known and loved is like smacking our heads against the lid of our jar. We stay confined in the place of being loved because we do not engage our will in being known. It's not about exercising enough will power to stop drinking, gambling, or the host of other addictive behaviors. If we spent half the energy on being known that we spend on being loved …

Wow. The universe might implode.

You can decide right now from which place you want to live your life. Do you want to be free to be the one God made you? Do you want to stop jumping through hoops? Are you done with being ripped off? Would you rather be known and loved instead of just loved?

If so, read on. There is more ground to cover in this mystery of identity theft.

5

THE ALLEGORY OF
THE CAVE

Like everyone else, you were born into bondage, kept inside a prison that you cannot smell, taste, or touch.

—MORPHEUS

THE MATRIX

Is not the dreamer, sleeping or waking, one who likens dissimilar things, who puts the copy in place of the real object?

—PLATO

THE REPUBLIC

My kingdom is not of this world.

—JESUS

The *Matrix* movies have reintroduced the concept of a spiritual realm. The existence of an unseen world beyond our physical senses was rapidly falling into disfavor in our post-modern, Western culture. Neo and Morpheus thrust it back into the public discourse on the end of a slow motion bullet.

The movies do a masterful job of distinguishing between the physical and spiritual realms. As smart as we may think we are in the twenty-first century, we aren't the first ones to think about this. As far as we can tell, the dichotomy of physical and spiritual has been around almost as long as man has walked the earth.

In his famous Allegory of the Cave, Plato suggests that what we are able to experience in life is only a shadow of an alternate, true reality. Plato sets his allegory within a discussion between Socrates and Glaucon. Socrates is explaining to Glaucon that the world we live in is like a cave. In this cave are prisoners who are bound in such a way that they can only see forward. In front of them is a wall on which shadows are cast from a fire that is behind them. Between the prisoners and the fire is a road. On this road is where the "forms" are held up so the prisoners can see each form's shadow as it is cast on the wall in front of them. From these shadows the prisoners try to discern the true nature of the forms. Socrates tells Glaucon that, to the prisoners, "The truth would be literally nothing but the shadows of the images."[1]

Plato believed that what we can interpret with our senses is only a shadow of the truth. The idea of a horse is more pure, real, and true than what we experience a horse to be. Similarly, the idea of freedom, honesty, justice, love, kindness, etc. are the true forms of reality outside the darkened confines of the cave the prisoners inhabit. Platonic thought does not stop in its dealings with the metaphysical side of reality. Plato boldly asserts that there is "truth," and that this truth resides outside of what we are able to apprehend and experience with our senses. This concept is clearly seen in an exchange recorded in Scripture.

After Jesus' arrest the Sanhedrin sent him to Pilate. Pilate then went back inside the palace, summoned Jesus, and asked him, "Are you the king of the Jews?"

> "Is that your own idea," Jesus asked, "or did others talk to you about me?"
>
> "Am I a Jew?" Pilate replied. "It was your people and your chief priests who handed you over to me. What is it you have done?"
>
> Jesus said, "My kingdom is not of this world. If it were, my servants would fight to prevent my arrest by the Jews. But now my kingdom is from another place."
>
> "You are a king, then!" said Pilate.
>
> Jesus answered, "You are right in saying I am a king. In fact, for this reason I was born, and for this I came into the world, to testify to the truth. Everyone on the side of truth listens to me."
>
> "What is truth?" Pilate asked.[2]

Jesus is clear. His kingdom is not confined to the shadowy, imperfect, physical world we see, touch, taste, hear, and smell. His kingdom is of a completely different nature. As finite beings we cannot apprehend even a small detail of his world much less its essence.

It is this world, the kingdom of God, that coexists right around us. It is there, but we cannot access it on our own.

Jesus not only tells Pilate this kingdom exists but that

there he is king. Jesus visited this imperfect world so we might know that the "real" kingdom exists, the spiritual realm that exists outside the cave. Jesus is saying, "The truth exists. I know because that is where I live. It exists in my kingdom, and I am the Truth."

Pilate, for whatever reason, personal or political, won't even entertain the idea of truth.

Truth. "What is truth?"

What irony it is that Pilate looks straight into the face of the Living Truth, asks, "What is truth?" and then walks away. What misery it must be to reject truth on the basis of fallible senses.

Unfortunately, humanity has immersed itself in a humanistic, relativistic rationalism that permeates every segment of our society. Only what can be weighed and measured with the scientific method or comprehended through mathematical equations and the principles of physics is considered to be true.

Plato and Jesus both would clearly have trouble with what passes for truth today.

It seems that whether it is *The Matrix* in 2000, Jesus in AD 30, or Plato in 400 BC, the general consensus is the same: What we see and experience in this world is only a shadow of the real thing. Plato's allegory of the cave and Jesus' teaching on the kingdom of God are devices that illustrate a higher truth. This truth is that there is another world outside the one we interpret with our physical senses.

This other world is where the true image of everything we know resides: true joy, true peace, true love, true fulfillment, true purpose, true freedom. Our world consists only of imperfect copies of these truths. We live as prisoners in a cave trying to make sense out of the copies.

As humans we live in a fallen, imperfect world. As Christians we live in this same shadowy, fallen, imperfect world, but have access to reality and truth in Christ. The question is: "How do we gain access to—and learn to live in—that reality?"

6
THE CAGE

Every form of refuge has its price.

—THE EAGLES
"LYIN' EYES"

Should you choose to test my resolve in this matter, you will be facing a finality beyond your comprehension, and you will not be counting days, or months, or years, but millenniums in a place with no doors.

—JOE BLACK
MEET JOE BLACK

And did you exchange a walk-on part in the war for a lead role in a cage?

—PINK FLOYD
"WISH YOU WERE HERE"

My friend Matt was feeling tired. He finally went to the doctor. The doctor asked him what was wrong. He said, "I'm really, really tired." After tests and other diagnostic tools were utilized the doctor said, "You have mononucleosis. Take these pills and we'll see you in six weeks."

The pills weren't working. Matt visited the doctor again. "What's the problem?" he asked. Matt said, "I'm still really tired and I have this big knot under my arm." After more tests the doctor said, "Oh, it's not mono. It must be"—are you ready for this?—"*cat scratch fever.*"

Matt got a different doctor.

A month later he was diagnosed with stage three, anaplastic, T-cell lymphoma. Hmmmm, cat scratch fever or cancer? That's a swing and a miss.

The problem with Matt's first set of doctors is that they were fixated on the symptoms and misdiagnosed the disease. When Matt's second set of doctors figured out what the disease was, they could then start dealing with the real problem.

Matt's story illustrates a huge misconception within Christianity. The misconception is that Sin and sins are the same. An even greater misconception is to believe that one or the other does not exist.

In Matt's case, lymphoma was the disease. Fatigue, fever, and swollen lymph nodes were the symptoms of that disease. Humanity has a disease. It is called Sin. Capital S-i-n. It is the single most destructive force in the universe. It is complete, total, and hopeless separation from God. Every bad thing in the world that we experience is a symptom of this total separation from God: murder, rape, suicide, loneliness, despair, child molestation, genocide, bitterness, hatred, war, envy, disease, and yes, even cancer.

Western Christianity has spent the latter part of this great age of enlightenment apologizing for this particular element of Christian doctrine. Granted, sin theology has been misused through the ages. In the hands of the overly zealous, I'm sure many have felt "condemned" when they were told they were "bad people."

Therein lies the problem. Biblical Sin theology has nothing to do with being bad or being good. Heaven is not for good people, and hell is not for bad people.

Scripture is unmistakable: Hell is for those who continue to live life separated from God. Heaven is for those who admit they are separated and let Jesus' work on the cross work for them. Let's not bicker about who chose whom. The boilerplate Christian doctrine is clear: "But God demonstrates His own love toward us, in that while we were yet sinners, Christ died for us."[1]

Whether we want to admit it or not, we were born into a cage. Paul, in chapters 3–8 of Romans, did a masterful job of outlining in detail what we in the church have treated like the uncle nobody talks about. He asks these questions: Are we—

Slaves to sin, or slaves to righteousness?

Unmarried, or married to Christ?

In Adam, or in Christ?

Locked in a cage, or free as a lark?

Paul is clear. It has to be one or the other. There is no opting out. Scripture does not let us say, "Oh, I just won't be a slave then." Paul is meticulous in his metaphor and passionate in making his point: We are born a slave to sin, unmarried, and under Adam.

Like fleas locked in a jar, we are all confined to a cage. We are locked in tight, completely separated from God and all that he has for us. Ephesians 1:13 plainly states that "when you believed in Christ, he *identified* you as his own" (italics mine). Quite literally, when you believe what Jesus did on the cross, God changes your identity. You are no longer a slave to sin. You are a slave to righteousness! You are no longer alone. You are married to Christ! You are no longer dead in the fallen line of Adam. You are alive in the glorious riches of Christ! You are free to be your true self, the one that God had in mind since the beginning of time.

Over the years I've heard many definitions of what identifies a Christian: a good person, a follower of Christ's teachings, someone who is "religious," a good church-going, God-fearing person. The list goes on. At its elemental level this verse defines the standard Christian doctrine of what a Christian is: someone who believes that the life, death and resurrection of Jesus Christ is the sacrifice that makes us right with God. That's it. Nothing else.

In Romans 4:3 Paul restates Genesis 15:6, "Abraham believed and God credited it to him as righteousness."

E. M. Bounds, in his thorough discourse on prayer, defines belief as "trust." This trust is "faith become absolute, ratified, consummated."[2] To believe something in our modern culture is to make intellectual agreement with it. But this is not the belief of the Bible. Even the "demons believe there is one God—and shudder."[3]

When my children were young and learning to swim, they would stand on the edge of the pool trying to get up the nerve to jump to me out in that big wide-open pool. No matter how much I tried to convince them that

I would catch them, they would waiver on the edge, looking at me, looking at the water, and then back again. Ultimately, the belief that they could trust their father to keep them from drowning would win out and they would jump.

While feet are firmly planted on the side of the pool, it's just intellectual assent. It's not trust until feet leave the pavement.

When you make that jump into the waiting arms of your heavenly Father, you are made right with God. When your belief moves to trust, God moves you. He moves you from slave of sin to slave of righteousness, from under Adam to under Christ, from being unmarried to being married to Christ. Trusting what Christ did for us on the cross moves us from one place to the other. We can't earn it, do it, or buy it. We can believe it and God does the rest.

The overwhelming weight of Scripture clearly states that we are born locked in a cage with absolutely no hope of getting out on our own. Faith alone in Christ's work on the cross unlocks the door of that cage. The key has been turned. The lock has been shattered. The door has been thrown open. We understand this.

We can even quote Scripture to prove how much we understand this: "If the Son makes you free, you shall be free indeed"![4] We have great celebrations. We make wonderful proclamations "Hallelujah! I am free! Praise God! He has set me free!"—all from inside an unlocked, wide-open cage. Technically speaking we are free. Functionally speaking, however, we are in exactly the same place. The locked door was a restraint that has now been removed. There is a complete and total lack of restraint. The door has swung wide open, yet there we sit in our cage wondering why this Christian life isn't all it's cracked up to be.

Over the years I have talked to hundreds of Christians about their faith. More specifically I have talked with Christians about their walk with Christ. Words like "fulfilling" or "satisfying" or "exciting" or even "challenging" do not come up very often.

"Good" and "great" were about as high as it went on the "ecstasy scale." There were the few times I did hear from someone who was fired up about his or her walk with Christ. But in context, it was usually from a "newbie" who hadn't figured out that life in the cage was as good as it gets.

As people described their relationships with God, I began to realize a hard reality: that's the way I would describe my own relationship with God. I began to feel like I was living in a bad rendition of "Night of the Living (Christian) Dead."

Maybe I was talking to the wrong people, but I don't think so. Whether it is a general sense of uncertainty, doubt, apathy or fear, there is a general malaise that runs through modern, Western Christianity.

As a result, many in the church resort to living a blended version of existentialism and Christianity. Existentialism supposes that our existence is the only thing that is real. There is no God, no purpose, no meaning. Christian theology, and likewise Christendom, rejects existentialism at this base level.

Since our existence is the only thing that is real, existentialism states that we can only add value to our lives by what we do. We can only create meaning in our lives by our actions. This is where modern Christian experience and existential thought begin to merge—unfortunately.

Raw existentialism doesn't differentiate between noble, worthy, unworthy, or ignoble actions. Actions will add or subtract to the overall quality of existence only by how the actor interprets those events and outcomes.

Some have described existentialism as like being thrown off a tall building the second we are born. Our life consists of the time we have before we are splattered on the ground below. As a result, life becomes an all-out grab for what we can snatch, grab, pop, snort, drink, purchase, or otherwise consume in the short time we have before we hit ground.

Does this sound like behavior spawned from a philosophical presupposition such as existentialism? Or is this what we see in the church?

David Kinnaman, president of the Barna Research Group wrote in *unChristian*, his piercingly perceptive work on how those outside the faith view Christianity:

> One study we conducted examined Americans' engagement in some type of sexually inappropriate behavior, including looking at online pornography, viewing sexually explicit magazines or movies, or having an intimate sexual encounter outside of marriage. In all, we found that 30 percent of born-again Christians admitted to at least

one of these activities in the past thirty days, compared with 35 percent of other Americans. In statistical and practical terms, this means the two groups are essentially no different from each other. If these groups of people were in two separate rooms, and you were asked to determine, based on their lifestyles alone, which room contained the Christians, you would be hard pressed to find much difference. [5]

Evidently, our cups do not runneth over.

If we are not satisfied, if we are not experiencing fulfillment in our Christian life, we automatically assume Christianity is defective. It doesn't occur to us that it's not the Christian faith, or Christ himself, that is falling short. Lack of fulfillment is not a shortcoming of Christ, Christianity, or the God of the Universe. It is the unavoidable outcome of staying planted in a wide-open cage. It is a direct result of identity theft. After all, if we believe life inside the cage is as good as the Christian life gets, why wouldn't we make a grab for anything and everything we can get? Unfortunately, we have. Statistics tell us "the church" doesn't look much different than the world in any meaningful way. This is due in large part to cage mentality Christianity.

The cage door is open. Technically speaking, we are free. Functionally speaking, however, there is no difference between staying in a cage that is locked or a cage that is unlocked. Existence is still confined to the same familiar place. We are still captives unless we walk out of the cage. Instead, we stick to interpreting shadows on the wall. The sailboat is grounded in the sand. The fleas are in the jar. Freedom isn't really freedom. The human heart has surrendered to just being admired but never known.

As you read this book, I ask you to be honest. It is perfectly legitimate to admit feelings of dissatisfaction in your Christian life. They are your feelings. If they exist they should be acknowledged. You are not the first one to feel this way.

U2 recorded a song in the eighties that reflects exactly this sentiment:

> You broke the bonds.
> You loosed the chains.
> You carried the cross and my shame, and my shame.
> You know I believe it.
> But I still haven't found what I'm looking for.
> No I still haven't found what I'm looking for.[6]

This theme has been echoed over the last three decades in many formats and mediums. I have had to come to a few conclusions in my life when it comes to "I Still Haven't Found What I'm Looking For" Christianity. I've had to ask myself a few questions before I came to these conclusions. They go something like this: "Self, do you really believe the God of the Universe funneled himself down into human form, stepped out of eternity into time, walked around in sandals, sweat, taught, lived life, took beatings, scourgings, and suffered a horrific death *as God incarnate* so my estrangement from God could be reconciled?" Then I had to ask myself, "Self, did God Incarnate experience that death so that he could be raised again into an eternal life that he offers to me via the Holy Spirit *who lives inside me*?" And finally I had to ask myself, "Self, is the Holy Spirit of the Living God of the Universe not capable of fulfilling one human soul?"

Put in those terms, "self" was convinced that if he wasn't being fulfilled it wasn't God's fault.

Again, feelings of discontentment are normal. We cross a line, though, when we blame God for our feelings of dissatisfaction. If you still haven't found what you're looking for it's because what you're looking for is *not inside the cage*. It's "out there."

A low budget "Night of the Living (Christian) Dead" experience is not the life God intended for us. I believe God is calling us out of our cages. It is there, outside the cage, that we will begin to understand freedom, love, joy, peace, fulfillment, and yes, even excitement. Following Christ out of the cage will reveal more of the idea, the form, and the truth because he is The Form. He is The Truth.[7] We can stay in our cages and settle for being loved, never knowing the freedom of being intimately known, or we can move out of our cages into life, freedom, wholeness, and deep, healing intimacy with our God.

7
T.O.M.D.O.S.S.

*The shepherd drives the wolf from the sheep for which
the sheep thank the shepherd as their liberator, while
the wolf denounces him for the same act as the destroyer
of liberty. Plainly, the sheep and the wolf are not agreed
upon a definition of liberty.*

—ABRAHAM LINCOLN

*I have become
comfortably numb.*

—PINK FLOYD
"THE WALL"

*This indecision's bugging me
should I stay or should I go?*

—THE CLASH
"SHOULD I STAY OR SHOULD I GO?"

My friend Koby and I moved into our dorm room at
Texas A&M University in the fall of 1983. Our room was
in Dunn Hall. The Only Men's Dorm On the South Side, or
T.O.M.D.O.S.S., as it was referred to with reverence by
the occupants, and disgust by everyone else. Room 326,

like most other college dorm rooms was … bleak. White cinder block walls on a white linoleum tile floor. This might be good for some but it was completely inadequate for a couple of suburban boys from northwest Houston. So we decided to fix it up. Paneling. Carpet. Comforters and the "bag monster," an oversized, incredibly comfortable, soft Brazilian leather beanbag chair that was the envy of the entire wing. After a little work and a lot of trial and error, we made our twelve-by-fifteen sterile box into a room that was really, really *cool*. Looking back, I probably would have made it to class a little more often if my dorm room had been a little more sterile.

Therein lies the problem with leaving the cage: We work so hard fixing it up, why would we want to leave? I mean, we've installed the ceiling fans and the flat screen home theatre with surround sound. The list goes on and that is not even the beginning of the plans we've made for our cages.

We have our friends. We have our sense of security. We have our place in the social order. We even have our theology. We pretty much have it dialed in. Why would we leave?

Sadly, many Christians will never leave their cages because they are comfortable. Behind comfort, though, lies control. Behind control is fear. Inside the cage we are in control. We know this. To move outside the cage is to lose control. That is too scary a proposition so we just stay put.

Something happens, though, when we stay planted in a cage with a wide open door. incongruity sets in. We know what we experienced with Christ when we trusted him with our lives. We learned Joshua "fit the battle of Jericho," "seek ye first the Kingdom of God"[1] and it was "for freedom that Christ has set us free."[2] Repeating these while sitting in our unlocked cages, though, brings an unsettling hollowness to those words. What we have learned about the Christian life is incongruous with our Christian experience. Incongruity causes stress. We all deal with stress in different ways. Unfortunately, most of the ways we deal with stress are not altogether healthy.

The longer we sit in our cage wondering why our experience doesn't match up with our expectations, the easier it is for the unholy trinity to seep in with those nagging little doubts. Abraham Lincoln sheds light on one in particular:

> The shepherd drives the wolf from the sheep for which the sheep thank the shepherd as their liberator, while the wolf denounces him for the same act as the destroyer of liberty. Plainly, the sheep and the wolf are not agreed upon a definition of liberty.[3]

What a great statement on the tension between staying in the cage or stepping out. Christ is the Good Shepherd who has come to liberate his people. The chains have fallen. The lock is broken. The door is open. There we sit perched comfortably in our cages engaged in an intense inner monologue over the nature of the Shepherd: liberator, or destroyer of liberty?

The Spirit whispers, "Liberator!" The world shouts, "Destroyer of liberty! Whatever is right for you is right! Anything else is just an antiquated moral code that will only bring guilt and shame!" The flesh says, "Destroyer of liberty! If it feels good do it! It's a victimless crime! Who needs all those stupid rules anyway?!" The enemy hisses, "Yeah, he's your liberator. Obviously he's not a very good one, though. I mean, seriously, look at your life. What do you really think he is?"

I love it when someone tells me, "As a Christian, if you're honest with yourself you feel _____."

Fill in the blank with the flavor of the month: Disappointed, unfulfilled, unsatisfied, un-whatever-you-don't-feel-at-the-moment.

The question presumes to know what I'm going to feel when I'm "keepin' it real."

Granted, modern Christianity seems to be permeated with a sense of unfulfillment. But that doesn't mean you have been sold a bill of goods! That doesn't mean that life in Christ is unfulfilling, disappointing, or unsatisfying.[4]

More and more it seems that Christian reality and Christian expectations are incongruous. Incongruity breeds doubt. Consistent doubt about the nature and the identity of Christ will kill any chance of a fulfilling and intimate walk with him. Your definition of freedom and fulfillment will change depending on your position. If you stay in your cage, you will come to view Christ as the destroyer of liberty; the one who has placed an unattainable moral code around your neck that only spawns guilt and shame in the face of a complete inability to meet its demands.

Staying in the cage condemns us to a life of hiding because the impostor, that part of you that has to hide behind the hand, feeds on the safety of the cage. We were born in the cage. We learned to fake it in the cage. We will continue to fake it in the cage because we have become comfortably numb. We have become content with being loved, admired, respected, mistakenly powerful, and completely unknown.

To step out of your cage is to see Jesus as Liberator. He is the original Freedom Fighter who brings a freedom far greater than a mere lack of restraint. Stepping out of your cage is self-liberating because "self" was created and designed for life outside the cage. It is only there that "self" will find true freedom because true freedom is not only the lack of restraint, but taking advantage of the reason the restraint was removed to begin with. *That reason is intimacy with God.*

In pursuing God out of the cage, he leads us on a life of adventure, discovering new things, and living new experiences. There is light and sunshine and trees and mountains outside the cage. There is a whole new landscape—a whole new life in intimate, personal relationship with God.

So your cage may feel warm and comfortable. You know where everything is. But there isn't really very much in the cage, and most of what's there isn't worth having.

So, what will it take for us to find our courage, let go of the comfortable, and take that leap of faith through the open door? There is no other way to leave the shadows behind. There is no other way to experience the life God has waiting for you.

The freedom that comes from walking with Jesus outside the cage is not free. The impostor, the one who lives hidden behind his hands, cannot live long under the withering need for dependency on God that living outside the cage will bring. It will cost you one layer of veneer after another. All those masks. All the bobbing and weaving. All the different hands you have put up to guard your heart have only diminished your God-given identity. Following Jesus out of your cage will de-laminate your soul layer by layer, until the only thing left is you.

We were never intended to stay in the cage and live the rest of our lives in the endless inner debate. The only answer is Christ, the Liberator. Any other thought fades in the distance the further we move from our cage.

We stay in our cages for all these reasons. We leave our cages for no other reason than that is what God desires. Jesus is clear. In John 17:3 while praying to his Father he says, "Now this is eternal life: that they may know you, the only true God, and Jesus Christ, whom you have sent." We leave because the kind of naked freedom God offers is not a spectator sport. You will have to leave your cage if you are going to enter into what God has intended for your life. When he intended you, he did not intend you to live your life as a sandboat parked on a sandbar. Neither did he intend you to live the life of a slave in the confines of an open cage.

Granted, you've got your place looking sweet with all the things you have accumulated over time. The best things in life, though, aren't actually things. The best things in life are the passion, security, vision, fulfillment, freedom, joy, and complete, total, and inexplicable satisfaction that spring from intimacy with God. The frantic, all-out grab for stuff is a futile attempt to divert our attention from the pain and emptiness of our estrangement from the father heart of God.

We may have our cages looking good but that could be the very thing that keeps us from experiencing God the way we have always longed to. We have bought the lie hook, line, and sinker that "he who dies with the sweetest cage wins," but we were built for intimacy with God.

As we will see, our leaving the cage is not a strong suggestion, it is a biblical mandate.

8

DON'T ROCK
THE BOAT

Do you love me?

—JESUS

JOHN 21:17

It took me awhile to realize something about the life of Christ. It becomes quite obvious that he was an incredibly sought after individual. The man was obviously operating with celebrity status by virtue of the amount of people that were constantly around him. Crowds were so crazy that at one point the disciples seem to actually be concerned about Jesus' safety.

We find in Matthew 14 that the crowds that were always around had followed him out to the middle of nowhere. It was late and the disciples wanted to know how the people were going to eat. Philip was getting a little antsy and pressed Jesus on exactly what his plan was. (Have you ever said something and immediately wanted to reel the words back into your mouth like they were somehow magically tied together with fishing line? I think that's what Brother Philip must have felt like when he questioned Jesus' plan.)

Jesus looked at them and said, "You're going to feed them." Amazingly, they did just that. With just a few fish and loaves of bread they fed at least 5,000 people.

It is wonderful that Jesus did this great miracle to feed all these people. What is more amazing is that he did it through the disciples. Jesus provided the endless supply of bread and fish, but the disciples executed the plan. Jesus could have performed this miracle in many different ways. He could have snapped his fingers and had a portion of food appear right in front of every person in the crowd. He simply could have declared, "You are full!" and everyone would have said "Mmmmmm, that fish and bread sure was good. I'm stuffed!" But that is not how he did it. The disciples did not sit around and observe food magically appearing on plates. Jesus told them they were going to do it, and they did it.

To drive this home, Jesus later tells Peter in John 21, "Feed my sheep." Even by Peter's own account, he failed dismally, yet Jesus directed Peter to actively lead and nurture the church. Henri Nouwen adds that Jesus' desire is that we engage with people as "vulnerable brothers and sisters who know and are known, who care and are cared for, who forgive and are being forgiven, who love and are being loved."[1]

The biblical imperative is clear. Jesus, if nothing else, was intentional about everything he did.[2] His intention is clear. He desires for us to be engaged in what he is doing in the world. Christianity was never intended to be a spectator sport.

If, after all this, Jesus' intent was not clear, it soon would be.

In my college days we set a fairly attainable goal for teenagers in central Texas: We were going to water ski at least one day out of every month of the year. It's Texas after all. People come from all over the country to enjoy the mild winter weather. Easy enough—until one day in February we got in way over our heads.

We had to borrow a friend's boat because the family boat was out of commission. It was a cool day but not unbearable with our wetsuits. But then in an instant, it all changed. In Texas, what we call a "blue norther" came screaming in over the lake just as we were about to trailer the boat.

Unless you actually have the experience it is truly un-believable. The speed with which events unfold is con-founding. The bottom drops out of the thermometer in an instant. The lake becomes a vicious, boat-battering tempest. The wind began screaming so loud we couldn't communicate with our loudest voices even when we were only yards away from one another.

I had borrowed the boat, so it was my job to trailer it. Steve and Tarik brought the trailer down to the ramp as I drove the boat out of the cove to meet them at the ramp. Unfortunately, the bow of the boat had to briefly face north—right into the jaws of the beast—before I could get it lined up with the trailer. The wind and the waves were so fierce it would lift the bow up so high that the outboard engine would dip under water and die.

After a few tries it became apparent that driving the boat onto the trailer was not going to happen. I jumped into the frigid water in order to swim the boat the remaining few feet to the trailer.

It was like a bad dream. Tarik had brought the wench cable to the end of the trailer so we could hook it on and wench the boat in. After a number of exhausting tries, we were inches away from a successful hook when another mammoth wave lifted the boat up and away from the trailer. The wind once again blew us away from the shoreline.

Completely worn out at this point, I began yet another attempt to swim into the onslaught of wind and rain. It was then I noticed that so much water had washed over the sides of the boat that the gas tank was floating around inside. A quick glance at the ignition confirmed that the key was switched on. As I pushed down on the back corner of the boat to switch the key off, water poured over the back corner. In a mind-boggling instant, the boat disappeared under the waves right beneath me.

Gone.

Yeah, that made for one awkward phone call to the friend who had loaned me the boat.

Not many people have the bright idea to water ski every month of the year. But then again not many people have the experience of being in a boat in a raging storm: sailors, merchant seamen, me and a couple of my buddies, and, oh yeah, Peter and the rest of the disciples.

As we saw in Matthew 14, Jesus worked through the disciples to feed the five thousand. Then, like it was no big deal, Jesus went off to pray. He sent the disciples ahead in a boat. Of course the disciples are caught out in the open water when a violent storm sweeps in. But Jesus sees them "straining at their oars"[3] and heads out across the Sea of Galilee … on foot.

I don't know if you've ever put yourself in the disciples' place in this story. How would you react if, during the middle of a raging storm, somebody came strolling up to your boat out in the middle of open waters? The disciples didn't handle it very well. Actually, they kind of flipped out.

Since I've experienced the stress of trying to keep a particular watercraft afloat during a raging storm, I'll go ahead and admit that I would flip out, too. But I cannot say that I would ever do what Peter did next.

Peter calls out to Jesus. "Lord, if it's you, tell me to come to you on the water."[4]

We know the end of the story. Peter gets out of the boat and becomes the only mere mortal in history who has ever walked on water. The point is not that Peter walked on water. The point is that Jesus said, "Yes" to Peter getting out of the boat. Jesus did not say, "No, no, no! Stay in the boat! It is far too dangerous out here for you! Wait there. I'll come to you in the boat!"

Our situation is not so different from that of the disciples. Like the disciples in their boat, we are in a cage. Non-Christians have no hope of ever getting out of the boat/cage. Their cage is still locked shut. Christians, however, have every chance in the world of getting out of the boat. The door to their cage has been thrown wide open. Unfortunately, many Christian people are miserable because they live a life of "freedom" in the confines of a cage with a door that is wide open.

The biblical imperative is clear. Jesus never called us to stay in the boat. Likewise, he never intended us to stay in our cage. Jesus doesn't even give us the option to stand up on the railing. Some Christians "live on the edge" so they can be "edgy Christians." Jesus clearly calls us to live our lives over the edge—not near the edge or on the edge, but *over the edge.* The life God intends for every believer starts beyond the edge.

The story of Hernán Cortés is well known. Cortés arrived off the coast of South America with enough men, horses, weapons, and supplies to conquer the entire continent. Soon after his arrival, he did a remarkable thing. As the story is told, he offloaded all the troops and supplies from the ships. He then formed his men on the beach facing the ships out in the ocean. Then in full view of all of them, he ordered every ship to be burned.

I've tried to imagine myself as one of those men. The mix of emotions as I watched my ship—my lifeline home—go up in flames and then sink beneath the water. How horrifying that must have been. How *motivating* that must have been.

The message was clear: There was no turning back. Move forward and fulfill your purpose as a soldier of Spain or scrounge around on the beach until you die.

We find ourselves in a similar place. Move forward, over the edge of life as we know it and into the life God has for us or we can stay put, milling around in our boats, color coding our fishhooks.

My hope is that we as Christians will follow our hearts over the edge, take Jesus by the hand, thank our boats for being the safe, warm refuges they were, then set them on fire and watch them sink.

G. K. Chesterton wrote that "the heart has reasons reason knows nothing of." Unfortunately, man seems to have written, "Reason has reasons the heart will never hear about." In the great love story between God and man, man has consistently intellectualized all his reasons for staying in his cage. Instead of following his redeemed heart out into a passionate love affair with his Lord, he shrinks back and considers all the reasons why that's a bad idea.

Unfortunately, there is an opportunity cost to staying in the cage. It's not a small cost either.

9

THE SWEDGE

Swedge. It's just one of those funny words that makes me laugh. Other than humoring me, the word does play its part in the English language.

In the landscape plumbing business, workers fit pieces of PVC pipe together to construct underground lawn sprinkler systems. Many times these pieces of pipe are of differing diameters. The piece of pipe that connects two pipes of differing diameter is called a swedge. My best guess is this piece of pipe doesn't "sweep" water from the larger pipe into the smaller, nor does it "wedge" the water into the smaller pipe. Thus, we have the clever designation, "swedge."

Welcome to the swedge chapter.

In the last few chapters you have been introduced to the concept of the cage and two of the biblical imperatives that call us to live outside that cage. The next few chapters will explore why God desires us to move out of our cages: intimacy with God, partnership with God, honesty with God, and the perspective of God. My deep desire is that this discussion is not theological or philosophical, but practical. I hope that in reading these chapters you will find something that will help you live your life over the edge, outside the cage.

10
THE TORN VEIL

What's the big deal? I'm a good Christian. I do my best.
I do my job, take care of my family, give to the church. I
do my part.

Well, living outside your cage has nothing to do with
doing your part. That is mostly because it's not about you.
It's about God and what he desires and intends for you.

I have asked hundreds of people why Jesus died on a
cross. In response I have heard hundreds of variations
of, "He died for our sins." That is not a "wrong" answer,
of course. But it's not altogether right, either.

Did Jesus leave the right hand of God, live as flesh and
blood, heal the lame, raise the dead, teach the truths of
God, be tortured and killed on a cross for our sins? No.
He didn't even die for Sin, that disease of rebellion and
separation we are all born into. Yes, his death is a substitute for the death that rebellious mankind deserves.

He died so we could be reunited with him in an intimate, eternal, adventure-filled love story of epic pro-
portions. The cross of Christ was inevitable in the eternal scheme of things. Dealing with Sin was needed, but it
was never the point. The cross of Christ was necessary

for dealing the deathblow to Sin and death so sinful man could be in the presence of a holy God for eternity. The cross of Christ, however, was never the point of the incarnation.

The point was, has, and always will be *relationship*—abiding, intimate *relationship*. That is God's great desire and intention for you and me. The brutality of the cross echoes out across two millennia: "I am dying to be with you!"

The depth of Christ's suffering sears into our consciences his desire for deep intimacy. If the cross speaks to anything, it speaks to the death of superficiality. This kind of suffering speaks to God's desire for "deep unto deep"[1] intimacy. This kind of suffering does not reflect God's desire for shallow relationship with his intimately crafted creation while the creation itself is emotionally tethered to a well-adorned cage. Life in the cage has conditioned us to interact with our Savior on well-appointed schedules, on our own terms, with minimum enthusiasm. Every lash of the scourge, every drop of the hammer, beats out a rhythmic chant of "deep unto deep, deep unto deep, deep unto deep."

There is no other reason for the torn veil but deep unto deep.

> And Jesus cried out again with a loud voice, and yielded up His spirit.
> And behold, the veil of the temple was torn in two from top to bottom; and the earth shook and the rocks were split.[2]

The veil. The fabric that separated unholy man from Holy God. The curtain that separated a holy sanctuary from the Holy of Holies; the place where God told Moses, "Here I am." That place of holy ground was so important David and Solomon built the temple around it. It was so sacred only one priest could enter one time every year to sprinkle the blood of a perfect sacrifice on the mercy seat, blood that represented the death mankind deserved. But God has revealed that his mercy triumphs over his judgment[3] and would take this substitute until the day the perfect sacrifice was made.

It was in the Holy of Holies that the veil was torn. It was there that the very presence of God was made available to all those who are in Christ. It was then that Solomon's temple became obsolete because those who "confess with your mouth, 'Jesus is Lord,' and believe in your heart that God raised him from the dead, you will be saved. For it is with your heart that you believe and are justified, and it is with your mouth that you confess and are saved."[4] The temple of God is no longer brick and mortar; it is flesh and blood. Christian, God lives in you! *You* are the temple of the living God of the Universe!

Nothing speaks of intimacy more than the tearing of that veil. God pushing away the shroud, beckoning with open arms as he whispers, "Come. Come in here to me, my beloved child."

If you were there at the very moment, would you stand back? Would you fall down in awe? Would you run into the very presence of God on earth? Or would you run as far away as your legs would carry you?

Granted the reality of that kind of intimacy with God is a scary—no, horrifying—prospect to many of us. I was absolutely stunted in my growth as a Christian because of my paranoid fear of being in the presence of God.

I couldn't imagine being in the presence of my heavenly Father because being in the presence of my earthly father was a place of judgment. It's not that my earthly father judged me at all. He was a successful doctor and a good father. He went to college when he was sixteen and was out of medical school at twenty-two. I was struggling out of my undergraduate degree at twenty-three. There was just no way in my mind that I could ever live up to what he was.

Like many of his generation, he felt his job was to take care of his family. He did that in spades. He was a hyper-provider. Unfortunately, that led to more of a business relationship between us.

I remember many times waiting on the edge of the couch as he went over my report card. They were straight A's some of the time—but not all the time, and I knew I just didn't measure up to my dad's expectations. And because I didn't measure up to his expectations, I didn't measure up at all.

The Word of God convinced me otherwise. The more I looked at, believed, and appropriated what God said about me, the more I realized I DID measure up. I did have what it takes—because God said so. It took a few years, but I gradually learned that being in the presence of God was not the same as being in the presence of my father.

I also learned that the authentic father heart of God is

not in the same universe as the apathetic, absent, or abusive hearts of our earthly fathers. As well-intentioned as our earthly fathers may be, they cannot know us intimately and love us perfectly as our Father in heaven does.

The torn veil is a symbol. Symbols are visual signs that represent some other thing. The torn veil does not represent God's desire for us to be dutiful, nice, or pious people. It does not represent God's desire for us to have perfect attendance at all church functions. Nor does it represent his desire for us to be faithful tithers. Again, those are all great things. By themselves, though, they miss the very essence of what happened in the Holy of Holies the day Jesus died.

The torn veil has stood through the ages as the symbol for God's desire for intimacy with his creation. I'm not Presbyterian, but the Presbyterians sure got it right in the Westminster Shorter Catechism: "The chief end of man is to glorify God and enjoy him forever."[5]

It is difficult to enjoy something from afar. A rose is beautiful from twenty feet away. But it is awe-inspiring when you are so close you can smell its sweet fragrance and see the detail of its petals and richness of its color. You might be able to appreciate it or recognize the aesthetic value of a rose from a distance. However, you cannot truly enjoy a rose from far away.

Inside our cages most of us truly do appreciate Jesus. I'm pretty sure, though, the incarnation, life, death, and resurrection of Jesus Christ didn't occur so we could join the Jesus Christ Mutual Appreciation Party.

Are you *enjoying* God? If you are, my bet is you left

your cage a long time ago. What is the fundamental reason why we appreciate God but don't enjoy him?

The cage.

Is God inside the cage? Yes. God is omnipresent. Unfortunately, all of your structures, crutches, and rationales for not throwing yourself with abandon into deep intimacy with the Lord are right inside there with you. Being omnipresent, he is also outside the cage. More importantly, what he has for you is outside the cage; what you have for you is inside the cage.

Simply stated, staying inside your cage makes you dependent on you, your ability to fake it and the constructs you have developed for making life livable. One of the lies the unholy trinity whispers to us is that God wants us dependent on him because he is a control freak who wants nothing more than to dominate every detail of our lives. The Christian life is reduced to a colossal, cosmic game of "Red Light, Green Light" or "Mother May I?" God is not a precocious child who derives some form of infantile pleasure from exercising oppressive control over his creation.

He really does have better things to do with his time.

Dependency on God is designed to bring intimacy with God. The entire point of moving out of your cage is intimacy with God. There is no other point.

Unfortunately, when it comes to moving, an involuntary reflex is tapped within us. It doesn't matter whether moving means getting up off the couch to do something for someone, or moving across the country because of a job transfer. Whatever the case, there is an innate tendency to draw back and weigh the options.

Part of that tendency is a God-given desire for self-preservation. The other element, however, is part of our brokenness. It is the desire to know "What's in it for me?" In the midst of logical calculation sits the sin of self-protection. Should we use the brain God gave us? Yes! Absolutely. In weighing the pros and cons of a situation, though, we are in danger of reasoning God right out of the picture.

Bishop William Willimon also makes an accurate observation about Western, egocentric Christianity:

> The modern, essentially atheistic mentality despises mystery and considers enchantment and befuddlement an affront to its democratic right to know—and then use—everything for purposes of individual fulfillment. This flattened mind loves lists, labels, solutions, sweeping propositions, and practical principles. The vast, cosmic claims of the gospel get reduced to an answer to a question that consumes contemporary North Americans, though it's hardly ever treated in Scripture: *What's in it for me?*[6]

What if, by moving out of your cage, there is absolutely nothing in it for you? What if, after weighing the pros and cons, the stack of pros is non-existent? What if, after generating a detailed profitability report, you are in the red?

Moving out of the cage does many things. The least of which may be a moving of Western, egocentric

Christianity towards authentic, Christo-centric Christianity. There is a place where "What's in it for me?" never crosses the mind of a Christian. That place, however, is not inside the cage.

When it comes to moving outside your cage there will be anxiety and very possibly fear. Henri Nouwen in his classic, *In the Name of Jesus*, writes about his move from Harvard University to Daybreak, a L'Arche community for the mentally handicapped. Nouwen, a highly respected Harvard educator and author was faced with moving from a job that kept him near the "burning issues"[7] of his time to a place where the most important question asked of him was, "Will you be home tonight, Henri?" Faced with living in a place where most of his training no longer served him, he writes:

> Not being able to use any of the skills that had proved so practical in the past was a real source of anxiety. I was suddenly faced with my naked self, open for affirmations and rejections, hugs and punches, smiles and tears, all dependent simply on how I was perceived at the moment. In a way, it seemed as though I was starting my life all over again. Relationships, connections, reputations could no longer be counted on.
>
> This experience was and, in many ways, is still the most important experience of my new life, because it forced me to rediscover my true identity. These broken, wounded, and completely unpretentious people forced me to let go of my relevant self—the self that can do things, show

things, prove things, build things—and forced me
to reclaim that unadorned self in which I am completely vulnerable, open to receive and give love
regardless of any accomplishments.[8]

Henri, God bless him, is writing about following God
out of the cage to a new place. It is exciting to me that
he experienced a "rediscovery" of his identity. Following
God out of the cage strips away the layers of pretense
and pride that have been built around our trusted
mechanisms and constructs. Henri is honest in saying
that great amounts of anxiety came with this process.
Anxiety is completely normal when it comes to moving
out. It is what God gave us to keep us from running off a
cliff without thinking it through first.

When it comes to fear, though, please hear this: God
did not give you a spirit of fear![9] If fear is involved in
moving out of your cage, it is not from God! It is not from
the Holy Trinity. It is from the unholy trinity. God did not
give you a spirit of fear. He gave you a spirit of "power,
and of love, and of a sound mind."[10]

Intimacy with God is the point of moving out of our
cages. The next few chapters will explore some of the
ways we can begin to realize deeper intimacy with God:
Honesty with God, the perspective of God, and partnership with God.

11
TREE FORTS

You have been weighed and you have been measured—and you have been found wanting.

—COUNT ADHEMAR

A KNIGHT'S TALE

God has made something better for us so that together with us it would be made perfect.

—HEBREWS 11:40

For we are God's fellow workers; you are God's field, God's building.

—I CORINTHIANS 3:9

God made him who had no sin to be sin for us, so that in him we might become the righteousness of God.

—2 CORINTHIANS 5:21

Some will read this book and think to themselves, "Yeah, this is all great but there is no way I'm getting out of my cage." The main reason many of us will never leave our cage is fear.

Fear of failure, fear of not measuring up, fear of being found out. Many Christians—men especially—never engage in Christian ministry because they fear that in the deep exchanges that ministry requires, everyone will see that they are shallow, unequipped, or unprepared at best. At worst, they fear they will be found out to be what every man fears at his core: inept, incapable, or incompetent.

These are real feelings. They can, and often do, drain every ounce of our desire to move out of our cage. Although the feelings are real, they are based in a colossal misconception. This is not a performance. God is not grading you on a bell curve by how well you do things in comparison to other people.

We believe we should bust out of our cage with a mind blowing, out-of-the-park performance. Then, if all goes well with our performance, we wait to see how God will grade us. We choreograph a gold medal routine: "I'll come out hard and fast into backward hand springs with a double backward layout and stick the landing. He'll be really impressed then."

He will. He will absolutely be impressed. He will love watching the performance. But it will leave you feeling a little empty—and God will feel a little sad.

The father heart of God is saddened when we come flying out of our cage, hair on fire, ready to get it done all by ourselves, because life is not one grand performance.

Life is not a performance because it is a partnership.

The concept of the God of the Universe desiring to be in partnership with me was so straight up whacked I could not grasp it.

Seriously, when you take on a partner in any endeavor,

the general idea is to pick someone who can help with the overall goals of the partnership; someone who brings something to the table. I don't know about you, but when I think of myself in partnership with God, I'm pretty sure I don't bring much to the table!

Think of yourself as a business consultant. I have come to your office to run my new semiconductor business past you for your professional advice. I give you my business plan, and you ask me what kind of business it is. I proudly reply, "It's a partnership." You say, "Well that's great! Who is your partner?" I say, "Well, my partner is … a monkey. He's a good monkey. He has great tree climbing skills. He makes people laugh with his funny tricks, and he's learned not to throw his poo at people."

You get the picture.

No one would go into business with a monkey. God, however, has gone into business with us. There was a time when I wasn't sure which was worse.

Then I learned the secret of the tree fort.

Our oldest son, Colton, had been after me to build a tree fort in the backyard since he was eight. By the time he was ten, I figured I'd held him off as long as possible. Besides, it was time for the man-child to learn about that hallowed right of passage to manhood: power tools!

This was going to be the first project that he would actually put his hands to. Accordingly, we sketched it out, made a list of supplies and made the journey together to the mecca of all that is male: Home Depot.

Upon our return from Man Depot, we set to work. Colton learned how to measure and cut plywood, drill two-by-fours, set four-by-fours in concrete, and nail real nails into real wood. After a few days of work, we had the real deal: a bona fide, although slightly out of square and not so level, tree fort.

There were times when Colton was operating the circular saw and it was not cutting along the line we had meticulously measured and drawn. Every time it happened there was this voice in my head that sounded suspiciously like my father's, telling me to "do it right or don't do it at all!" Consequently, there was a time in my life when I would have taken the saw from Colton and done it myself so it would be "done right." After all, my fingerprints were all over this project. Suddenly, it was no longer a father-son project; it was a monument to my manhood. If the final product turned out lame, that would reflect poorly on me. It didn't matter that my son and I were making memories. What mattered was that the end result was something that reflected my masculine prowess with manly tools—and stuff.

I'm happy to report that I kept my paws off the circular saw and our tree fort has now served its purpose for many years. It has been a platform for many a water balloon fight and Air Soft war but has mostly served as a launching pad onto the trampoline below, and all of this without falling down. Although it has functioned well, it is not the picture of perfection in construction engineering.

Herein lies the secret of the tree fort: It's not the product. It's the process.

Maybe our tree fort wasn't square and the floor

drooped a little to the left, but it was perfect. It was perfect because Colton and I did it together. It was perfect because we laid our hands on something together. As a result, what did not exist now does. What we could only see in our minds now stands up strong in our backyard. The memories of father standing behind son steadying his hand as he made his first cut with a power saw will be with us both forever.

That's the secret of the tree fort and the lesson I believe God wants every one of us to learn: It's not the product. It's the process.

Most Christians won't step foot out of their cage because whatever they do won't be good enough. It won't be perfect.

Hebrews 11:40 says, "God has created something better for us so that only together with us would they be made perfect."

Did you hear that?

"… *only together with us would they be made perfect.*"

It is no accident this verse is placed at the end of its chapter. It is the perfect finish to what has been known throughout Christendom as the "faith chapter." Hebrews 11:40 finishes off a hall of fame list of the great saints who worked in partnership with God. Whatever it is God has created for you to do, it will not be perfect to God until he is doing it with you!

I hope that completely blows your mind because it definitely blows mine.

Be certain of this, though: Sitting in your cage is not the thing God has created for you to do.

It is a clear biblical imperative: God wants you to sail straight out of your cage onto the high seas of life where you will have to trust him on a daily basis. Why? Be confident that it's not because he needs you to save the world.

How many times have you heard how God needs you to get involved because the world is going to hell in a limousine? Yep, me too.

God calls us out of our cages because it is there that we will grow in intimacy with him. I know of no other way to see growth and change in life than to move into deeper and deeper places of intimacy with God. Don't be confused, though. Your growth as a person or even as a follower of Christ is not the point. *Intimacy with God is the point*. Your growth is a by-product of intimacy with God.

How many times have you heard that to be a good Christian you must read your Bible, go to church, do good things, and pray? All those are great and necessary things! But I believe our souls cry out to be intimate with God because that is the place we are known and loved. Read your Bible? Yes! But read your Bible because it will lead you into a deeper, intimate knowledge of the one Holy God! Pray? Yes! But pray because it will lead you into a conversational love relationship with God!

Remember the secret of the tree fort! It is the process of being in partnership with God. We will be perfected when we venture out of our cages and into intimacy with God. As we are being perfected, we will mark this imperfect world.

God does not need you. He desires you. There is a big difference between need and desire. He desires intimacy with you, his precious, wonderful, beloved child. But as long as you are in your cage, "it ain't happ'nin' girlfriend."

As much as you think you are going to go deep with God sitting in your cage—you're not. You may be a great Bible scholar, you may have memorized hundreds of verses in your cage, and yet never have intimacy with God because you don't have to trust him.

Doesn't a lifestyle of living in sin start with mistrust? We don't trust God to meet our needs so we meet them outside the will of God. That is a great definition of sin.

Scripture memory is imperative for the Christian life. The Word of God is eternal, life-giving, and it transforms the human heart. It was never meant to be hoarded by well-intentioned Christians who believe they will "study" their way into the deeper things of God. The Word of God must be committed to the purpose of God. The perfect purpose of God is intimacy with his creation. It must be put to work outside the cage before you will grow into a deep intimacy with God. Besides, the gospel works best in the place where "sinners and tax collectors" live. You don't have any of those living in your cage with you, do you?

Biblical "head knowledge" is not the same as experience with God, just as knowing about God is not the same as knowing God. You will only gain experience with God in a viable, two-way partnership *outside* your cage.

Partnership with you is God's desire. It is in this day-to-day relationship that the process of intimacy takes place. A performance mentality puts the spotlight on us. It focuses all the glory on us when we succeed, but it also shackles us with guilt when we fail. We were never designed to go it alone.

Partnership with God brings intimacy with God. In relational evangelism there is a time-tested adage: see, talk, do. In establishing a relationship with a complete stranger, you must first be seen. In our ministry to high school kids, we show up at high schools. As I once heard Woody Allen say about his craft, "90% of good acting is just showing up." It is the same with relational evangelism: 90% of relational evangelism is just showing up. Once you have hung around long enough, you will begin to talk to people in a very natural, spontaneous way. Talking is how people begin to get to know each other. After talking with someone for a while, it is time to do something with them. In our ministry, this could be going to the mall, engaging in some kind of sports activity, going to the beach, etc. We also employ weekend and week long camping trips. Spending a 24/7 with someone really lets you get to know them.

Doing something with someone deepens relationship with them. Doing something with God will deepen your relationship with him. Doing something with God will require you to get out of your cage because God is not in the interior design business. He's in the transformation business. He's not interested in the product because it is during the process that we are drawn into deeper intimacy with him.

There is a cage. God is calling us out into an intimate partnership with him. Some will go. Some will not. Many who stay will stay out of a misguided sense of self-importance. Let's face it: Some of us, as we will see next, take ourselves way too seriously.

12
RULES OF LIFE

Lighten up, Francis.

—SERGEANT HULKA

STRIPES

Christ and him crucified ...

—1 CORINTHIANS 2:2–4

*... God's weakness is stronger than the greatest of human
strength.*

—1 CORINTHIANS. 1:25 (NLT)

*Brothers, think of what you were when you were called.
Not many of you were wise by human standards; not
many were influential; not many were of noble birth. But
God chose the foolish things of the world to shame the
wise; God chose the weak things of the world to shame
the strong.*

—1 CORINTHIANS 1:26, 27

Bill Butler is one unique individual. I've known Bill for many years. Our jobs have kept us in touch intermittently over the last two decades. If you spend any time around Bill you will soon know about "Bill Butler's Rules of Life."

Bill's first Rule of Life is: "There is a God and I'm not him." The second is: "Your mother is always right." Everyone would do well to adopt Bill's Third Rule of Life: "I'm not cool."

I have.

It is wonderful when you can just say it out loud: I'M NOT COOL!

I could be doing you the biggest favor of your life by telling you this: You don't have it all together. Go ahead, say it out loud: "I DON'T HAVE IT ALL TOGETHER!" Wow. Can you feel that? Can you feel the weight of self-importance, the need for people to think you have it wired, rising up off your shoulders? Freedom: wonderful, blessed, blissful freedom.

That kind of freedom only comes from one place: honesty with God. We were born in a cage but we insist on living our lives trying to convince ourselves and anyone who will listen, "Those aren't bars. That's not a lock. Move along! Nothing to see here!"

The apostle Paul may be the quintessential example of someone who left the cage. When I read his letters, I am continuously struck by the way he refers to Jesus. It is warm, personal, devoted, reverent, passionate, and any other word that would further describe *intimate*. And even in the midst of this deep, abiding relationship with the Lord and the résumé he brings to the table, he still writes, "I came to you in weakness and fear, and with much trembling. My message and my preaching were not with wise and persuasive words ... but Christ and him crucified."[1]

Paul not once relies on his extensive track record in the mission field or his blue chip status in the fact that Jesus personally "recruited" him. No.

"Christ and him crucified."

"That's all I got."

One night I was helping my twelve-year-old with his math homework. It was late. He had been going all day. His mind was mush. He was stuck on one very simple thing. After going over it quite a few times, he just looked at me and said, "Dad, that's all I got." There are times when we have to say, "That's all I got." When you get to that place, it's just time to pack it in.

Unfortunately, we don't start from a place of emptiness and dependence on God. We start at the drawing table carefully choreographing our grand performance. We detail out how we will impress God because we are uber-cool, uber-talented, uber-rich, uber-funny, or just plain uber-uber. If you think, thought, or ever start thinking that any of those things are going to win brownie points with God, you would be uber-wrong!

Performing comes from a need to know that surely we've got *something* going on. Granted, you do have something going on. I know this because you are a one-of-a-kind, amazing, special creation of God himself. In our Christian culture there is a tendency to drift to one end of a spectrum. On one end of this spectrum are the performance junkies. I know them because I am a re-covering performance junkie myself. On the other end of the spectrum are the ones who subscribe to something I call "worm theology."

Worm theology says that apart from Christ we are pathetic, worthless losers. We must prejudicially reject anything that says human beings created in the image of God are anything less than precious, valuable, and worthy. Christian, non-Christian, Muslim, animist, outright pagan is not the point. Human life is a miracle that should be valued in any body it inhabits. If God thought anything else, he would have washed his hands in the flood and been done with us.

There is a kernel of truth in worm theology, but at its extreme this viewpoint becomes self-loathing, out of balance, and unhealthy. Apart from Christ, we are stuck in a cage. Apart from Christ, we are powerless. Apart from Christ, we have no hope for living the life God intends for us. This, however, does not make us worthless. It makes us even more priceless in the face of Jesus' suffering on the cross.

If we are such dirty, lame, worthless creatures, why would the God of heaven go through everything he went through? Why would he even get off the couch much less funnel himself down into a human body so he could endure a brutal and humiliating death? It is clear. God obviously believes you and I have immense value. If what we feel like is very far away from what God says about us, something is amiss.

We are neither worthless, pathetic losers, nor are we self-sufficient masters of our own universes. What we are is redeemed children of God, having all we need for every good work in Christ Jesus.[2]

Some of us believe we are made for greatness in Christ

but there is that "thing" in our lives that keeps us from experiencing the life God has for us. Many have unilaterally "DQ'd" (disqualified) themselves from working in partnership with God.

Some feel they must have fifty verses memorized or read the Bible through ten times before they can do anything with or for God. Others feel like they have nothing to offer because they don't have a knock-your-socks-off, "gutter-to-God" testimony.

Whatever "thing" you have going on, you need to know that you are never DQ'd from intimacy with God. Intimacy with God is not reserved for monks, priests, pastors, and the religiously devout. The father heart of God is as equally open to the drug-addled, alcohol-drenched, guilt-, pain-, and shame-ridden people as it is to the "doin'-fine-today-praise-Jesus-thank-you" people.

Many Christians are beaten down spiritually because, in the midst of a sincere commitment to Christ, they feel if they were "good Christians" they wouldn't struggle with a particular sin or habit.

First, let's review. Just as hell isn't for "bad people," heaven isn't for "good people." Since heaven isn't for "good people," the intimacy God offers isn't reserved for the "good Christians." Intimacy is the overarching desire God has for all of his creation.

Second, we need to distinguish between "things" that are merely bad habits versus things that are sinful. Biting your fingernails is different from cheating on your taxes. Using caffeine to wake up in the morning is different from using porn on the internet. Engaging in "overshare" is different from gossip. Being negative is different from being drunk.

The upside is, regardless of what the "thing" is, the presence of God is open to all those who are in Christ. The downside is that sin separates.

Sin separates you from others. That's why the "doghouse" exists. And I don't mean the house the family pet sleeps in. I'm talking about that metaphorical place we find ourselves in when we have broken trust with someone in word or deed. Distance is created, and/or grows, when we gossip, cheat, steal, lie, or otherwise break an implied or explicit trust between us and another human being. It is a spiritual law. Sin brings death, separation, and distance.

Sin also separates you from *you*. In chapter 4 we saw how and why we hide behind an artificial self, putting our hands in front of our faces, so to speak. I lived behind my "church hands" for a long time so no one would see my doubts, my pain, or my struggles. After all, I was a leader in Christian ministry. I couldn't afford to have dirty problems like all those non-believers. There was tremendous internal and external pressure to keep life on the rails of the "Perfect Christian Express." As a result, my true self was becoming more and more alienated from the "church hands" image I was projecting. The more distance I was experiencing between my pretend self and the person I knew I really was, the more I was convinced God was powerless to change me.

Praise be to God that he convinced me otherwise! Much of my journey through God's gracious and gentle convincing is recorded in this book. I no longer hide behind "church hands," or any other combination of hands for that matter. I have found freedom and complete and total contentment in the fact that God DIGS me just for who I am. Because I am convinced at my core that he loves me without all my bells and whistles, I no longer live a fractured, estranged, compartmentalized life.

Finally, sin separates you from God. Yes, in Christ you are no longer separated from God. But as Paul wrote in Romans, "The wages of sin is death."[3] Remember that when Paul is writing to the Romans, he is writing to the Roman Christians. Historically, the Romans 3:23 text has been reserved for showing non-Christians that they are doomed to a life of eternal death and separation from God without Christ. Paul, however, is admonishing Christians. He is telling them the simple truth: Sin will bring distance between you and God because it brings death with it.

I'm pretty sure I don't have to tell you this. You know this. I know this. When we mess up, the last thing we want to do is go get intimate with God.

The question is asked all the time: "So, when you are 'intimate' with God, you become 'perfect'?" Re-stated, the question is, "So you won't struggle with sin anymore in this intimate relationship with God?"

There is a direct relationship between growth as a Christian and depth of intimacy with God. Can that be statistically proven? Probably not. Have I grown to treat my wife with more love and respect as I have grown in intimacy with her over the years? Yes! Do I want to serve her more and say no to myself more because of my love and commitment to her? Yes! Did I force myself to change my behavior? No. Did I make decisions differently as I moved into a deeper awareness of who she is and what she means to me? Yes. This dynamic is one of the great object lessons God would love for us to learn from marriage. Behavior changes in the face of authentic, intimate, loving relationships.

Our preoccupation with becoming "perfect" is just another glaring spotlight shining brightly on egocentric, performance-oriented Christianity. "Ooooh," some may think, "intimacy with God is the next bandwagon to jump on. This will be the thing that gets me over the hump."

No! Intimacy with God is the point of Christianity. It is what God is and has been doing for thousands of years. We have made it about something completely different. We work hard to find the antidote for our "thing." We read the Bible more, we go to church more, we pray more, we get more counseling, we take different meds, we read the newest book, we stop doing said "thing" for thirty days, we make deals with God, etc.

While we are running ourselves ragged looking for the cure for our "thing," God looks at us and loves us.[4] Again and again he softly, lovingly calls from the Holy of Holies, "Come in here to me, child. This is my desire."

But while God calls, we continue making up stuff to do like a child who has learned to ride his bike with no hands. The first few times your child says, "Look, Mom! Look, Dad! No hands!" It's cute and wonderful. After twenty or thirty times, though, it's not so cute.

Hopping on one foot while juggling and simultaneously singing "Camptown races sing that song, doo-da, doo-da," might have been cute the first time. Although impressive, after the twentieth time it's not so cute anymore. Let's admit it. At that point, we aren't so much trying to please our parents, God, or anybody else. We're just showing off. In our relationship with God, sometimes our behavior isn't for God anymore, it's about us.

Do we think God is so mesmerized with our juggling act that he doesn't notice the "things" in our life? I have stood in my cage executing my juggling act with gusto and precision. Then, as God's glance started to drift from my very impressive performance to that "thing" down in the corner of my cage, I would juggle *faster* and sing *louder*. "'CAMPTOWN RACES SING THAT SONG!' Hey, God! Hey! Look over here! 'DOOOOO-DAAAAAA!' No! Nooooooo! Not over there! Over here! 'DOOOOO-DAAAAAA!'"

Henri Nouwen says:

> The great word that we have to carry as ... followers of Jesus, is that God loves us not because of what we do or accomplish, but because God has created and redeemed us in love and has chosen us to proclaim that love as the true source of all human life.[5]

In the midst of our junk, with all of our "things," all we got is Christ and him crucified. That's it. That's "all we got."

Honesty with God is essential for getting out of the cage. It is essential because there is no intimacy without honesty. Relationships do not work when there is dishonesty about behavior, thoughts, fears, passions, and beliefs. Any relationship with God has to start with honesty. You will not experience growth in your relationship with God if: 1) You are not honest with yourself about who you really are, 2) You are not honest with God about who you really are, and 3) You are not honest with others about who you really are.

Men and women alike have the things they refuse to be honest about. Men, Christian men especially, talk about living with integrity. Integrity has become the one-word summation of all that defines the dutiful Christian man. The first definition of integrity is, "*The quality of possessing and steadfastly adhering to high moral principles.*"[6] Men are very comfortable with that definition because they can do, strive, reach, or attain a state of being that reflects that definition. Remember the Christian existentialism we talked about in chapter 6? We add value to our lives only by what we do. I used to believe I was adding value to my life by "living with integrity." In the end, though, it became death because it was an attempt to live up to a moral code imposed on me, by me, and those around me.

The second definition of integrity is more alien to men and women alike. That definition is, "*The state of being complete or undivided.*"[7] The root of "integrity" is "integral" or "integrate." To "integrate" means to bring two or more things together so they make a larger whole.

Remember the hand in front of the face, the impostor, the one who desires to be loved but lives completely unknown as a consequence? You exist, but you exist behind a persona that you want everyone else to think you are. To live outside the cage is to integrate the real you with the "church-friend-job-spouse-family-hands" you.

There are different ways to accomplish this. I, for one, didn't really experience an integration process. I simply killed the impostor. I refused to be something I wasn't. I came to a point where I was simply done with living somebody else's life. It wasn't pretty. It was quite messy actually, but I have no regrets about that time in my life.

Allowing God to take me to a place where I could be honest with myself brought a completely new dimension to my life. God-ordained honesty has allowed me to live free from the fear of being "found out." When you live in this freedom, relationships are no longer threatening because there is nothing to hide. Instead of things to be managed, relationships become vehicles that take you to wonderful places of intimacy with God and others.

So while we're being honest, let's just say it: We're not cool. We don't have it all together. Actually, a lot of us have some bad habits, but God's weakness is far stronger than the greatest of human strength.[8] Let go of your needs to be powerful, respected, admired, relevant, and loved, and lean into the eternal, unfailing, surprising strength of God. Instead of focusing on what you can do *for* God, focus on what God wants you to do *with* him. In our desire to have it all together, we completely rob God of the entire purpose of the cross: holy, sacred, deep, communion with his precious creation.

Being honest with God will bring a whole truckload of git-over-yerself with it. Getting over yourself will bring a new perspective on many things. It may even bring a new perspective on perspective.

13
PERSPECTIVE

You don't have a soul. You are a Soul. You have a body.

—ATTRIBUTED TO C. S. LEWIS

I came home from work one day to find out that it had finally happened. After weeks and weeks of pulling, twisting, turning, and otherwise messing around with it, our oldest finally lost his first tooth. The day he had been looking forward to with great anticipation had finally arrived. It didn't materialize quite the way he had it envisioned, though.

He was climbing up the ladder to the swing set in the backyard. One of his friends was just ahead of him. Unknown to Colton, his friend stopped at the top of the ladder. In an instant he face-planted right into his friend's bottom. Other than his wounded pride, the only casualty of the incident was his first loose tooth, which somehow came flying out of his mouth and vanished under the swing set.

"Vanished" might be too strong a word. It was more like looking for a needle in a haystack made of needles. The ground in that part of Austin, Texas (where we were living at the time), is black clay mixed with bits of white shale. I know some folks have never seen shale. So for you who have never experienced it, I'm thinking of a way to describe it to you. How should I describe it to you? Hmmm. Oh, I know. It looks like tiny bits of white teeth—thousands of bits of teeth all scattered beneath the swing set.

Since Colton was so excited about losing his first tooth, I was fairly obligated to initiate a completely doomed recovery mission. If you didn't know this already: Men don't "find stuff." We "initiate recovery missions."

About thirty minutes into my quest, however, I began thinking about how to couch my impending defeat to the firstborn. Should this be a lesson in dealing with disappointment in life? Maybe I should go with the "Ah, c'mon. It's a just a tooth, right?" approach.

As the reality of failure began to sink in, I began to pray "Lord, I would love to come out of this looking like 'the man' for finding this tooth, but I really would just love for Colton to have his first tooth."

It seemed like only a nanosecond later when something came to me. It wasn't an audible voice. Some may call it intuition. Others may call it a hunch. But when you are praying for a direction and an instantaneous answer comes out of the clear blue, it's hard to say, "Nah, that's not God. That's just a hunch."

At the moment I "heard" God I had been on my hands and knees for about forty-five minutes. I was slowly picking my way across the "needlestack" in a southwest-to-northeast direction. Like someone dropping a penny in a wishing well, this thought was simply dropped into my head: "You need to change your perspective."

I thought, *Ha, ha, ha. "Change your perspective." Yeah, that's funny. There are thousands of tiny tooth-like pieces of shale out here. "Change your perspective." Like that's going to help. What does that mean, anyway?* I wish I could say I was so confident that I heard God that I got up and immediately changed my perspective. However, that was not the case. Reality said I was running out of daylight and was rapidly facing the prospect of facing Colton with the bad news. Sure, he would live through the disappointment, but "change your perspective" kept coming back to me.

The sun was officially down. I was working off the residual light of dusk having a discussion with myself on my hands and knees in my backyard looking for a really, really small tooth. In the big picture of life with wars, genocide, famine, terrorism, and disease, does God really care about this tooth?

It was then that I agreed with myself (and God) and came down squarely in the affirmative: Yes, God does care about the small stuff. He is actually big enough to care about the big things and the little things.

I promptly swung my legs around approximately 180 degrees so I was "changing my perspective" by traveling northeast-to-southwest. Immediately—as in the first thing I looked at—I found the tooth.

A change of perspective is due if you plan on living life outside your cage.

In addition to intimacy with God, partnership with

God, and honesty with God, gaining and maintaining an eternal perspective is an integral element of living life outside the cage. We need to change our perspective!

Here's a saying that will help you do that: "You don't have a soul. You are a Soul. You have a body."[1] As simple as that statement is, it carries deep implications for our day-to-day lives. As Christians, we agree with this statement in principle. In practice, however, we seem to believe we are bodies first that merely have souls as part of the package deal.

Our focus is constantly drawn to things that speak to the physical. Billions of dollars in advertising are spent every year with that purpose in mind. Television, radio, billboard, internet, and magazine ads are all vying for our attention. Advertisers so want us to believe that we need a juicy hamburger, we need a sweet car, or we need to wear certain underwear, shirts, or jeans to be beautiful.

The amount of sexual imagery we are exposed to is astounding. Madison Avenue has understood for a long time that sex sells. Sex sells because it appeals to the flesh, that part of the unholy trinity that works to keep you in your cage. Using sexual imagery at an increasingly repetitive pace has an outcome. Any coach or athlete will tell you that repetition is foundational to good training. Repetitive exposure to sexual imagery may be a non-issue to some or a lustful stumbling block for others. What it trains all of us to do, however, is to focus on the physical. Advertisers want to convince us that we are physical bodies in need of being catered to by their clients' products. How many products would we buy if advertisers were trying to convince us we are souls that have a body?

The body speaks to the physical. The soul speaks to the spiritual. Staying in the cage keeps you reliant on the physical world. What you can see, do, achieve, etc. Moving out of the cage makes you dependent on what you *cannot* see. That is why Hebrews 11 defines faith as being "certain of what we do not see."[2] The word "certain" does not translate into "I think God can" or "I'm pretty sure God can." That is a cage mentality. That is what we think like inside our cage. No, "certain" means "I know God will."

Do you look beyond the physical? We all need to. Could God be doing something through that really irritating person at work? Would God save you from a bad situation by delaying that flight for two hours? Is there a reason you could be waiting in that line for so long? Are you going to Home Depot just to pick up some home improvement items?

My friend Brett Rodgers isn't.

Brett is a Zen master when it comes to seeing the spiritual behind the everyday things we do. He keeps a sticky note on the dashboard of his car that simply reads, "Focus on the spiritual." I've known Brett since college. Since I've known him for that long, I can tell you Brett is someone who has developed and maintained an eternal perspective.

A trip to Home Depot for Brett doesn't usually end up with just a few new home improvement products. A recent trip ended up with the employee who was assisting him confessing, "Yeah, I've been out of the church for a long time. Maybe it's time for me to go back."

That may not be earth-shattering ministry to you, but God's not looking for earth-shattering ministry. He's looking for people who love him and love people well. Brett loves people well. That is why total strangers talk to him about things that matter.

You don't have to lead someone to Christ in the middle of Home Depot to love people well. If you decide you want to love people the way God loves people, you're going to have to trust me on this one: God will provide you with many opportunities if you are willing.

If you have any desire to move out of the cage, a change of perspective is due. Instead of the physical, begin to ask God for the eyes to see what is going on in the spiritual. Yes. There is a matrix, but it doesn't exist because Hollywood made a movie about it. It has always existed. Hollywood just noticed it a few years back. If you are willing, God will begin to reveal the spiritual realm behind the physical world.

An eternal perspective will come in handy when you begin to use a wonderful gift God has given you. Let's unwrap this gift together in the next chapter.

14

RECONCILIATION

All this is from God, who reconciled us to himself through Christ and gave us the ministry of reconciliation.

—2 CORINTHIANS 5:18

But you are a chosen people, a royal priesthood, a holy nation, a people belonging to God, that you may declare the praises of him who called you out of darkness into his wonderful light.

—1 PETER 2:9

Some will read 2 Corinthians 5:18 and think that to move out of the cage means "doing ministry." I've been asked many times: "Do you really believe *everyone* has a ministry?" My immediate answer is, "No, not every*one* ... but every *Christian* has a ministry."

Let's break that down. Most people believe that "doing ministry" will land them in a pulpit or in a hot, desolate foreign country with no friends, no food, and no skills, which may sound a lot like hell to most people.

Those thoughts, however, would be misconceptions.

Scripture is clear. When God reconciled us to himself, he

gave us something. I'm going out on a limb here, but I'm going to say that getting something from God would be a gift of immeasurable value. So when Scripture says God has given us something we should pay very close attention.

Born in a cage: Zero dollars.

Life lived in intimacy with God: Completely fulfilling.

Gift from God: Priceless.

What is this gift God has given us? It is the ministry of reconciliation.

> Therefore, if anyone is in Christ, he is a new creation; the old has gone, the new has come! All this is from God, who reconciled us to himself through Christ and gave us the *ministry of reconciliation*: That God was reconciling the world to himself in Christ, not counting men's sins against them. And he has committed to us the message of reconciliation.[1]

We have seen that it is God's desire and great joy to work in partnership with us. It is the process not the product that he is interested in. We may have our foot on the accelerator, but God's got the wheel. The ministry of reconciliation is the vehicle in which we reach the destination: intimacy with God.

You have a ministry: a God-ordained ministry of reconciliation. A process God is inviting you into that he will use to reconcile his creation to himself. All you have to do is show up.

"Well." I can hear it now. "My faith is a very personal matter." Horse hockey! However you want to label it—private, very private; personal, deeply personal—Scripture does not allow for a private faith. Faith in Christ was designed to be lived out in the community of Christ and the world at large. At this writing I have yet to find one single Bible verse that could lead me to believe my faith belongs in a closet. "Hide it under a bushel? *Yes!* This little light of mine I'm *not* gonna let it shine?" That is not how that song goes! It's time for Christians to come out of the closet! It's time for the church to move out of the cage!

As Christians, we are reconciled to God through Christ. As we have seen, God has given us the ministry of reconciliation. The term "reconciliation" in the Corinthians passage clearly indicates a third party. This third party is the world (the inhabitants of the earth.) If the Christian faith was supposed to be a private affair, maybe God would have given us something like "the ministry of self-improvement." He didn't.

Every Christian, male, female, young, and old alike have been given the ministry of reconciliation.

"Well, what about the little old lady who can't get out anymore?" Yes, there are physical and sometimes mental limitations at play. However, the scriptural imperative still stands. Besides, there are many "little old ladies" who can make killer chocolate chip cookies for shut-ins. I've known a few "little old ladies" who were monster prayer warriors.

In fact, Jim Rayburn, the founder of Young Life, always said he didn't "found" anything. He said that several "little old ladies" in Gainesville, Texas, were praying for high school kids for a year before he showed his face in town to start what became Young Life. In the decades since then, Young Life has reached millions of kids all over the world. Don't put your limitations on God—those "little old ladies" in Gainesville sure didn't!

Many Christians believe they are doing God a favor when they put money in the offering plate, give to a good cause, or otherwise "do good things." Somehow, we have this idea that the wheels are going to come off if we don't help God out.

It is time to figure out a pretty simple truth: God doesn't need us. Let me take that out of the plural: God doesn't need you. He doesn't need me. The fact that he desires to work in partnership with us does not confine him to only working with us. He can and will work right around us for his purposes to be realized. The question is: What are we missing out on when God goes around us?

Intimacy with God is what we miss out on. God doesn't need you. He desires you. Because he desires intimacy with you he has given you the ministry of reconciliation. It is a gift that will lead you to deeper places with the Gift Giver.

You have a ministry of reconciliation. What does it look like? Read on.

15
MEAT'S IN THE STREET

I gave you milk, not solid food, for you were not yet ready for it. Indeed, you are still not ready.

—1 CORINTHIANS 3:2

Gentlemen, this is a football.

—VINCE LOMBARDI

When you have your first child, you can find yourself becoming seriously neurotic about your child's development. Doctors don't help this. When your infant hits a certain age, you are supposed to take the brand-new child in for his or her first well-baby checkup. At the time our first child was born, I had no idea what a well-baby checkup was. If you've never lived through one here is a brief description:

The nurse comes into the treatment room with a clipboard, a pen, and quite the disapproving look. She then launches into a battery of questions about the "wellness" of your baby. I've had final exams that went better than the well-baby checkup.

After every question we would give a fairly confident reply. Nurse Feelgood would then make some unintelligible muttering sound and scribble something on the paper and continue with the interrogation: "Are you breast feeding? Is he off formula yet? Has he had any solid food? Is he pushing himself up yet?" I was completely unaware I could become defensive so quickly: "Yes. I mean no! I mean, I don't know! Are they supposed to be doing push ups at three months?"

I didn't know I was supposed to study for well-baby checkups. After a few more checkups, I became much less neurotic and realized Nurse Feelgood really wasn't the devil. She was just concerned with our baby's development.

Being a parent, I have experienced well-baby check-ups, potty training, first steps, and the first trips to the emergency room as part of our children's development.

Being in vocational ministry, I have witnessed the spiritual formation of many. I have made a few observations about this thing we call spiritual formation. Most of these observations culminate in one overarching theme: The meat's in the street.

As we have seen by Nurse Feelgood's well-baby exam, one of the markers to a child's development is moving from milk or formula to solid food. Development for the Christian is no different. Paul says, "I gave you milk, not solid food, for you were not yet ready for it. Indeed, you are still not ready."[1]

Paul is simply saying, "I preached the gospel to you. You received it. You are a new creation in Christ, a baby.

Since you are babies, I did not give you spiritual meat; I gave you spiritual milk."

In the same way, parents don't come home from the hospital with their brand-new bouncing baby and say, "OK, Junior, here's the remote, there's the fridge, here's the phone. Call if you need us. See ya."

New Christians need to be fed in order to develop spiritually. That is clear. The problem is not *what* they need to be fed, but *how* they need to be fed.

The church has been committed to the idea that all spiritual development will occur within the church walls. There have been numerous battle cries of many churches proclaiming, "Equip the saints!" We spend hours hearing sermons, sitting in Sunday school classes, adult Bible fellowships, and home groups so that we may be properly equipped.

In our seminaries, spiritual formation is an academic discipline. Budding Christian leaders can take many classes that teach people how to grow spiritually. Stay in seminary long enough and one could even get a doctorate in spiritual formation. The discipline of spiritual formation itself is not the problem, though. It is essential and has made great contributions to Christian life.

Modern spiritual formation has erred by attempting to grow Christians while they are still inside their cages. Knowledge does not equal maturity. Knowledge along with experience will bring maturity. This experience with God will not happen inside the cage.

I can hear the grumblings already. "Silly, silly boy. You have a valid point, but it is much too ... simplistic."

There's that word again.

It's springtime. Picture yourself in one of the most hallowed places in all professional sports: Lambeau Field in Wisconsin. You are a new recruit for the Green Bay Packers, and this is your first day of practice. The whole team gathers around one figure at the center of the field. It's Coach Vince Lombardi.

As a kid, you heard the stories. You may have seen the great moments in Green Bay Packer history. As one of the greatest coaches in sports history is about to speak, you find yourself leaning in towards this icon of leadership knowing that the words will be life-changing at best, worthy of his great stature and reputation at the least. It grows silent. Coach Lombardi lifts a football high over his head and says:

"Gentlemen, this is a football."

Wow.

Gentlemen, this is a football? Are you kidding me? Arguably one of the greatest coaches of all time and all we get is, "Gentlemen, this is a football"?!

Yes. We get, "Gentlemen, this is a football," because Vince Lombardi knew the secret of great football: blocking and tackling. Blocking and tackling. Blocking and tackling. He was so committed to the basics, he was not intimidated by holding a football over his head in front of some very big, burly men who were practically born with a pigskin in their hands and telling them very directly, "Gentlemen, this is a football."

Vince Lombardi may not have known it, but he also knew the secret of spiritual formation: Keep your head up and your butt down, and you'll do fine. We have become so fancy with all our methods and formulas about how we are going to infuse spiritual growth into the body of Christ that we have missed a basic point.

Let's admit it: We know how to be much better Christians than we already are. If Christians could just get the basics down, the world would be a much different place.

Hmmm. That begs a question. What are the basics?

Once again, I've heard many answers to this question. Instead of listing them, let us go straight to the source.

In Matthew 22 we find Jesus in a tussle with the Pharisees.

> Hearing that Jesus had silenced the Sadducees, the Pharisees got together. One of them, an expert in the law, tested him with this question:
> "Teacher, which is the greatest commandment in the Law?" Jesus replied: " 'Love the Lord your God with all your heart and with all your soul and with all your mind.' This is the first and greatest commandment. And the second is like it: 'Love your neighbor as yourself.' All the Law and the Prophets hang on these two commandments."[2]

There it is. The basics of the Christian life according to Jesus: Love God. Love people.

In the last chapter we saw that we all have the ministry of reconciliation. The ministry of reconciliation starts right here. Love God. Love people. When you begin to love God with all your heart, mind, and soul, you will begin to see people the way God sees them.

Eugene Peterson in his excellent paraphrase of Colossians 1:28 writes, "We preach Christ, warning people not to add to the Message. We teach in a spirit of profound common sense so that we can bring each person to maturity. To be mature is to be basic. Christ! No more, no less."[3]

Maybe the question is harder than you think. Maybe the question is not, "What are the basics of Christianity?" nor, "What is my ministry of reconciliation?" The real question is: "Do you love God?" Are you engaged with, infatuated by, absorbed in, hopelessly committed to, and willfully submitted to the living God of the Universe?

Don't be confused. Many have been beaten about the head and shoulders (in a Christ-like way, of course) with "Thy holy stick of the Great Commission." Yes, we need to carry out the Great Commission (Matthew 28:19–20). The Great Commission, however, does not supersede the Great Commandment. That's why Jesus said, "This is the greatest commandment."

Do you love people well?

Husband, are you loving your wife well? Child, are you loving your parent well? Pastor, are you loving your congregation well? Christians, are you loving non-Christians well? Better yet, are you loving other Christians well? Employer, are you loving your employees well? (Yes, that can be done even in this day of crass expediency.)

In loving God you will love people for a very simple reason: because God loves people. In loving people, you will be doing the Great Commission. Simple.

We can say we love God all day long. Those words are hollow until we are ready to move out of the cage and love God with our lives and not just our words.

I've observed something else about spiritual formation. My friend Grover Pinson recently summed up this observation. In his sermon, "The End of Burger King Christianity," the Right Reverend Pinson wondered why most Christians had no motivation to study Scripture, have a regular devotional, or just live the Christian life in general.

The conclusion to this great sermon was that most Christians don't study Scripture, spend time with the Lord, or just generally grow in their faith because, in fact, *they don't need to.*

By and large we are all living in our cages where it's nailed down and dialed in. Why would we study the Bible when we never have the occasion to put it to use? Why would we approach the living Word of God like our lives depended on it when they don't? Why would we run to God with the hardship and pain of bearing another's burdens, when we can't remember the last time we bore someone's burdens? Why would we need to rely on God to be our eternal source of life after we have poured ourselves out in his service, when we haven't poured ourselves out? We don't need to be poured into because we are never poured out.

We miss it.

We miss those tiny little sentences that are all through the Gospels:

"… he went up on a mountainside by himself to pray."[4]

"… Jesus got up, left the house and went off to a solitary place."[5]

"Jesus went out to a mountainside to pray, and spent the night praying to God."[6]

"… Jesus often withdrew to lonely places and prayed."[7]

"… and he said to them, "Sit here while I go over there and pray."[8]

Look at these excerpts in their context, and you will see something more profound than prayer alone. Jesus got up early and spent time with the Father because the Father was his source. In and around these verses, he is doing stuff. Big stuff. Not little stuff.

Walking on water.

Raising the dead.

Facing his own imminent death.

Jesus spent time with the Father because it was there that he revitalized his connection with the father heart of God. He didn't spend that kind of time praying because it would enable him to do great things. He spent that time because he loved his father and wanted to be with him. Out of that intimate love relationship came an amazing capacity to love people well. Jesus performed miracles because he loved the people that those miracles benefited.

Yes, the miracles he performed confirmed his deity. Jesus did not perform miracles, however, just to prove a theological point. He healed leprosy because he loved lepers. He gave sight to the blind man because he loved the man. He raised Lazarus because he loved him and his sisters, Martha and Mary. Miracles came from the loving father heart of God. Proving his identity was icing on the cake.

Jesus lived a rhythm of pouring out and filling up, pouring out and filling up, pouring out and filling up. Many Christians don't fill up, much less pour out. If we do fill up, it becomes a rhythm of filling up, filling up, filling up. Then, when we find the time, we pour out because it makes us look good, feel better, or it will help God out.

Living out your ministry of reconciliation can't be done inside the cage. The "street" part of "the meat's in the street" is the outside of the cage. Living out there will not always be easy, but it will always be good. It will be good because God will be changing you from the inside out. It will be good because you will discover things about the real you all along the way. It will be good because the impostor will gradually be dying away. It will be good because you will learn things about God himself. It will be good because God will always do more *in* you than he ever does *through* you. It will be good because you will become more like Jesus. When you live the gift of reconciliation you will know what intimacy with God is. You won't have to read a book about it, do a Bible study on it, or hear a sermon about it. You will know it.

"Oooooooh, yeah. I just don't think I have it in me. I mean, I'm a pretty busy person. I am scheduled to the hilt. If I stack on one more thing, I think I may just flame out."

I hear you. But please hear this: Loving people well is

not something you do. It is something you are. Your ministry of reconciliation is not a set of things you do that creates a certain outcome. Remember the secret of the tree fort. It's the process, not just the product, that God is interested in. Just as Jesus was, you too will be poured out in the process of loving people well. But here is another simple truth: Being poured out is different from being burned out.

Burnout comes from a familiar place. That place inside our cages that keeps us working overtime for the approval of others so we can be loved. Burnout comes from constantly changing the configuration of our hands in front of our faces so we can win all the kudos. Burnout is a direct result of identity theft. Burnout is the summation of running and working, running and working, running and working to win the admiration of our peers and the approval of God, even though we don't need the former because we've always had the latter.

The secret is out. Are you tired of swilling on milk in the confines of your cage? Do you want to grow spiritually? Then you need solid food.

Move out.

The meat's in the street.

16
GROUND CONTROL
TO MAJOR TOM

Houston, we have a problem.

—JIM LOVELL, APOLLO 13

Now it's time to leave the capsule if you dare
… I'm stepping through the door
and I'm floating in the most peculiar way.

—DAVID BOWIE

"SPACE ODDITY"

Don't fence me in.

—COLE PORTER AND BOB FLETCHER

"ADIOS, ARGENTINA"

We're all familiar with the famous words uttered by Jim Lovell during the near tragic Apollo 13 mission: "Houston, we have a problem." The disembodied, rehearsed, cool tone of voice belying a potentially epic tragedy is still unnerving to hear decades after this famous near miss.

The thought of floating off into space to certain death

by uncertain means is a horrifying prospect. To be drifting in space cut off from all your bearings, your direction, your way back home, is truly unimaginable.

Having grown up in Houston, I know that "Houston" means something to the men and women who fly into outer space. Although the Apollo rockets were launched at Cape Canaveral, Ground Control was in Houston. All the information, experience, and technology that kept the command module tethered to its course were in Houston. Staying connected to Houston meant staying connected to life.

Moreover, all astronauts live and train in Houston. The Clear Lake/Bay Area on the south side of the city is where their families and friends lived. Being disconnected from Houston meant being disconnected from everything they knew and loved.

While flying the command module, no astronaut in his or her right mind would knowingly cut ties with Houston. If they did, life as they know it would end. It may take days. It may take only hours. Either way they will die.

Astronauts depend on Houston to be in control every second of every mission. Without being completely connected to Ground Control, even a minute navigation error could mean the difference between success and failure. In the economy of space flight, that is the difference between life and death.

In everyday life, most of us don't live on the edge of living and dying. But we do live on the edge of life as we know it and life as God intended it.

As we have seen in previous chapters, God has "made something better for us so that only together with us would they be made perfect."[1] We have seen that we were born in a cage and that trusting in the epic display of grace through Christ's life-giving sacrifice, the cage door has been thrown open. Furthermore, we have seen that many of us will never venture outside that cage for a number of reasons.

Although the biblical imperatives clearly exhort us to live outside the cage, we stay put. Inside our cages we are convinced that it's better to be loved than known, it's all about the product not the process, our value is equal to our performance, and freedom is the lack of restraint. Inside our cages we are convinced that roses are red enough, peace is peaceful enough, joy is joyful enough, and intimacy is intimate enough. Ultimately, we have bought the lie that says, "How you experience God inside your cage is enough."

Clearly, there is no statistical data that will prove my point. My position is overflowing with personal experience and anecdotal evidence. Good luck trying to dispel the truth of it, though. We were created for something better than life inside the cage. The human heart cries out for it. Scripture declares it.

Even in the midst of the yearnings of our deep heart, we devise complicated intellectual arguments that rationalize our cage mentality. Over time we even figure out how to spiritualize those rationalizations. We don't stay in the cage because of deep, complex intellectual arguments. We've seen in chapter 11 that we stay in our cages out of fear. Here is another reason why we live life in our cages:

Control.

Intellectual arguments and excuses are only smoke-screens intended to cover up our deep need for control. It is that simple. We want to be in control. We like fixing up our cages. We want to have the final say on what we do with our time and how we spend our money. We want our FREEEEEEEEDOM!

"Hell," as C. S. Lewis put it, "is the greatest monument to human freedom."[2] God has always given us the right to choose. But we choose our way straight to hell because we want to be totally free of any restraint. We are much more concerned with our freedom than with close, intimate, personal relationship with God.

The truth is, we love to control stuff. We like to think it makes life easier. It is more convenient to push that button than to raise that garage door manually. But at a deeper level, we like being in control. As human beings we are infatuated with controlling things: doors, lights, TVs, circumstances, even people. Just give us something—anything—and we will try to manipulate it because it helps us continue to believe we are in control.

I'm in control, ergo I'm free.

Because you are hungry and decide, "Hmmm, I think I'll go make a sandwich," does not mean you are in control of your life. Exercising free will does not a master of the universe make. The reality of it is this: We are *not* in control. Our lives are out of our control. Our lives will be out of control with God or out of control without

God. That is the reality we face. Frantically scurrying around inside our cages trying to convince ourselves of our freedom by repetitive acts of free will not change this reality.

That is exactly what C. S. Lewis is getting at. Hell on earth exists. It exists in the form of the ridiculous things we do to pacify our misinformed ideas about freedom— one self-absorbed act of free will after another. Put together across the wide expanse of humanity it all becomes a seething, boiling cauldron of gnashing, gnawing, grabbing, groping, hell stew. Left unchecked, the raw energy of human lust for money, power, position, and possessions will only result in a furious, white-hot fire of rage against life unfulfilled. Perpetually fueled by the habitual need to self-medicate with still newer ways to find fulfillment through unadulterated acts of free will, this fire will burn until it consumes everything.

Sounds like a snapshot of hell to me.

Other than total immolation by self-absorption, a wrong idea of freedom keeps us completely pre-occupied with … the wrong idea of freedom.

Maybe, as I asked back at the beginning of this book, freedom isn't what we think it is at all. If we believe freedom is the total lack of restraint, then a question must be asked: "What would it mean to be totally free?" This means freedom from every restraint.

Just as an exercise, let's imagine we could free ourselves from every restraint. This exercise would assume that we move away from the little nuisances that tend to get in our way, like jobs, time, money, obligations, etc.

Being totally free from any restraint would mean we are even free from time and space limitations like gravity, inertia, and entropy. We could exist in the past, present, *or* the future. We could fly or jump hundreds of feet at a time.

We would have no physical limitations. We would never be sick because, after all, illness is a limitation. We would have perfect coordination because clumsiness is also a limitation. We would never forget anything because we would have perfect recall.

We would have limitless wealth. We could have sexual relations with anyone, anytime, anywhere. And of course, we would never die because death is the greatest restraint of all.

If all this could be possible *and* all of this could be possible *simultaneously*, we then might be able to entertain the idea that the total lack of restraint could bring fulfillment.

Of course all of this is *not* possible because we are finite human beings. Because we are finite human beings, we will coexist with restraints of all kinds.

So then, one might be resigned to think, "fulfillment is not possible in this life." That would be correct if fulfillment was a function of free will, but it is not. The question is not "Are there restraints?" It is a ridiculous proposition to continue believing we can free ourselves from restraints. Because of our mortality, our "finiteness," there will always be restraints. Since restraints exist we must face the music: We are not in control. Therefore, the question is, "In the face of restraints, do

I believe the exercise of my free will is going to bring fulfillment?"

As surely as we believe life is in our control, it is not. As we have seen, the question is not, "Am I in control of my life?" The question is, "How am I going to live this out-of-control life? Will I go it alone or will I go with God?" Maybe it's time to give up our romance with free will and start asking, "Since free will cannot bring fulfillment, what, if anything can?"

Christians, we have a problem. By staying in the cage we are continually insulating ourselves from our Ground Control. At the very least we are trying to fly the ship while at the same time fighting the very thing that will keep us connected to life. We live our lives like an astronaut who has disconnected himself from his Ground Control and is flying around in space because he just doesn't like the imposition of being restrained.

Walking out of the cage is an admission to God that we are not in control, and we are going to stop acting like we are in control of our lives. Just as the astronauts of the sixties and seventies had to rely on Ground Control for their very lives, God is beckoning us to rely on him with the same kind of belief, investment, and trust.

If we could lay down our free will for just one minute, I wonder what could happen? If we could resist the deep-seated temptation towards the frenetic exercise of free will, could we get a glimpse of the life-giving, inherently safe, and very reasonable limitations God has laid out for us?

The proverbs say, "There is a way that seems right to

a man, but in the end it leads to death."[3] If we pursue un-bridled free will as the way to fulfillment, it will lead to doubt, frustration, and death. An honest look at my life forced me to the conclusion that I had a dysfunctional relationship with free will because I mistakenly believed it was the vehicle that would deliver fulfillment. I was wrong. I was wrong because fulfillment is not a result of free will. I was wrong and I realized I had to start asking myself a different question.

So where is freedom? Where is fulfillment? Are these cozy notions reserved for the philosophers, idealists, and utopians? I don't believe so. I believe Scripture speaks plainly about these issues. The next chapter will explore what many Christians have never considered or, more sadly, stopped believing.

17
MA'GAL

Along the road your steps may stumble.
Your thoughts may start to stray.
But through it all, a heart held humble
Levels and lights your way.

—DAN FOGELBERG
"ALONG THE ROAD"

There are numerous references to the idea of "plenty" in Scripture. Passages such as, "the riches of his glorious inheritance," or "the unsearchable riches of Christ" in Ephesians are a couple among the many. Although, the concept of filling or becoming satisfied is referenced throughout the Bible, I am not advocating that Scripture should be read through the lens of what relationship with God should or could be doing for us. This is especially true in the context of material wealth. Material wealth has absolutely no bearing on any conversation concerning intimacy with God.

With that in mind, Western, egocentric Christianity has convinced itself it has been ripped off because it doesn't live in a constant state of "fat-'n-happy."

Once again, if we have "fulfillment issues," that's not on God. That's on us.

One of the most beautiful expressions of fulfillment in Scripture comes from the Psalms.

> You visit the earth and water it,
>> You greatly enrich it;
>> The river of God is full of water;
>> You provide their grain,
>> For so You have prepared it.
> You water its ridges abundantly,
>> You settle its furrows;
>> You make it soft with showers,
>> You bless its growth.
> You crown the year with Your goodness,
>> And Your paths drip with abundance.
> They drop on the pastures of the wilderness,
>> And the little hills rejoice on every side.
> The pastures are clothed with flocks;
>> The valleys also are covered with grain;
>> They shout for joy, they also sing.[1]

Wow. God's paths *drip* with abundance. God's paths do the dripping, not our paths. If our paths drip, they drip with the consequences of human self-interest. God's paths drip with *abundance*. This verse certainly does not say, "If you follow God's paths you will be fulfilled."

Or does it?

God is boldly declaring that his paths drip with abundance. He is inviting us to his banquet table, where his banner over us is love![2] Can you begin to imagine the spread at a banquet put on by God himself for you, his beloved? Can you smell the roasted meats, the breads, and candies? As naked, starving, and needy as we are in our cages, there is a feast waiting. If we sit and dine with God himself until we are stuffed to the gills, can we say that God's abundance is not enough? Would we be able to say that God's abundance is not fulfilling?

To say that God's abundance is not enough is haughty, prideful, arrogant, and rebellious. Fulfillment in this life is only going to come from God's abundance. It will not come from our over-zealous attempts at milking free will or working to impress God or trying to make others love us.

Some very well-meaning Christians have given up on abundant life simply because it is not their experience. Many have made arguments against the idea that Christians should hold out hope for a fulfilling life in Christ. I believe this is happening because 1) there is confusion between the ends and the means of freedom and fulfillment, and 2) Christendom has become devoid of any serious talk about obedience.

And Your paths drip with abundance.

Implicit in the term *path* are a few associative terms that need to be looked at: narrow, safe, and convenient. First, a path is not a boulevard or a superhighway with ten different lanes to choose from. A path, by definition, is extremely narrow. It requires the traveler to choose. Paths are not an all-inclusive proposition. A path is an exclusive means to an intended destination. There may be other paths to an intended destination, but the traveler must pick either path A or path B. Once on path A, path B has been excluded as a means to the intended destination.

Second, implicit in the word *path* is safe. Paths exist because they are proven avenues that guide through nuisances (i.e., thorn bushes, poison ivy, etc.) or dangers (ledges, crevasses, etc.). If a traveler were to leave a particular path, there could be adverse consequences to those actions. Ask any soldier who has had to follow a path through a minefield. In terms of safety, choosing to stay on the path will bring outcomes that are greater than arriving at a destination (i.e. you actually arrive … intact and breathing.)

Finally, the idea of convenience is associated with the word *path*. A path is convenient because traveling through a rain forest on a well-worn path is exponentially better than bushwhacking through the jungle on your own. Following a path takes much less time and energy out of a traveler than meandering around through uncharted territory.

Some of us, at some level, have issues with all three of these meanings when it comes to following God's pathway.

Although we mostly like the idea of staying on a path because it is safe and convenient, we rebel against the narrowness of it. We refuse to see that it is safe and convenient precisely because it is narrow. Oh, how we feel so constrained when we are faced with the mere proposition of forcing ourselves onto a narrow path!

The consequences of straying off God's path are synonymous with the consequences of sin. Bad things happen when you stray off the path in the middle of a minefield. Bad things happen when you stray off God's path in the middle of life.

I can already hear the collective uproar, "Oh, really?! So bad things don't happen to Christians who follow God's paths?!" Unfortunately, because we are broken people and we live smack in the middle of the aforementioned "hell stew," we suffer the consequences of the freewill-a-palooza going on in our lives as well as the world around us.

But again, do we want to live through problems we bring on ourselves, or the pre-ordained trials God has and will set before us for his purpose? Trials are conflict. More pointedly, trials are conflict with God. We will not experience intimacy with friends, spouses, children, or God without healthy, biblically resolved conflict. The trials we face on God's paths are part of a great predetermined, pre-ordained purpose.

A Christian who desires the path of God will have conflict in life. It is a necessary tool God uses to shape us into the image of Jesus. Conflict, trials, and hardship are only unnecessary when you and I look like Jesus. Do you look like Jesus?

I don't.

Some of us aren't so sure God's path is safe. To take this to its logical end means, of course, we don't believe God is safe. We don't believe his plans are to prosper us,[3] but to bring us harm.

As far as bushwhacking goes, some of us really believe (and I mean really, really, really believe) that God's ways are so much more inconvenient than our ways.

Even when we add up all the pain, heartache, frustration, emptiness, discontent, and outright harm we have doled out and experienced as a result of bushwhacking on our own, we are still convinced that our way is so much easier and convenient than God's way. We are world-class bushwhackers. Machetes in hand, we will spend pounds of energy in sweat and tears just to say, "See God, got here all by myself!" All the while we ignore the gaping wounds and scattered carnage we have accumulated on the way.

Narrow, safe, and convenient accompany another word we don't like much. *Obedience*. If, in the church today, sin is the uncle nobody talks about, obedience is the red-headed stepchild no one will acknowledge as their own. The word "path" implies obedience. Obedience requires submission to restraint. This restraint, we believe, hinders our free will. And when our free will is impinged we believe that will lead to a life unfulfilled.

The psalmist says, "God's paths drip with abundance"— not pain, agony, danger, inconvenience, disillusionment, or unfulfillment.

The Hebrew word for path is *ma'gal*.[4] This word refers to furrows in a field made by carts as they are being pulled by calves during the harvest. This is such a great picture of what God is telling us. Furrows, or trenches, are clear markings of where a cart or wagon has traveled. If you could shrink yourself down and jump into one of these small trenches, you could follow it with ease for the entire distance the cart has traveled.

Interestingly enough, within *ma'gal*, there is a

connection to the abundance and "fullness" of the harvest. Putting yourself in the middle of God's furrow, God's path, brings abundance. An abundant life is a fulfilled life. God's paths drip with abundance.

Obedience is abundance.

Now that we have established the right connection between free will, obedience, and abundance, let's finish with the reason why God wants us in his furrows.

It's not because he is a gianormicus control freak. It's because he's smarter than we are. I know that to a number of readers this will come as a real shock, but it's true. God really is smarter than we are. Because he is smarter, he knows that there are some things that we as humans will just refuse to believe. Namely, we will refuse to believe that God's constraining, irritating, narrow little pathways are actually leading us somewhere.

God's paths drip with abundance because they lead us to deep intimacy with our creator who loves us so much he funneled himself down (talk about constraining!) into the likeness of a human so we could live life and life to the full. God's paths lead us into life-giving, itch-scratching, soul-satisfying intimacy with the one who thought up life to begin with. All along the way we are fulfilling God's great desire that we look more and more like his beloved, majestic, passionate, beautiful son, Jesus.

The path of God leads us to intimacy with God via the character of Christ. In this process the great bonus to us is *LIFE*.

"The thief does not come except to steal, and to kill,

and to destroy. I have come that they may have life, and that they may have it more abundantly."[5]

This may be the most overused, and yet most grossly underestimated, verse in the New Testament. It is underestimated because we fall short in our estimation of what *life* is. It is underestimated because we try to fit adjectives on *life* that we have never truly experienced. Living in our cages talking about abundant life is farcical. It is ridiculous. It is akin to a single, never married television reporter attempting to capture the essence of a married couple that has lived out an epic love story for decades. She couldn't do it in a two-hour special, much less a two-minute human-interest story on the nightly news. It can't be done.

It can't be done because, first, we tend to "report" only the good stuff. We talk about the dates, proposals, honeymoons, sex, companionship, acceptance, babies, the first steps, first A's, first touchdowns, goals, perfect scores, graduations, etc. Secondly, the bad stuff doesn't usually make the highlight reel. We don't report on the disease, depression, estrangement, unemployment, addiction, unfaithfulness, or financial and emotional hardships.

The good, the bad, and the ugly, are part of epic love stories. There is no way to truly know peace until you have lived through turmoil and upheaval. True joy is not fully felt until it is experienced alongside gut-wrenching sorrow. There is no healing without brokenness. All of that is part of abundant life because it is part of the epic love story our creator desires to live with us!

But we move around inside our cages with hands covering faces, jumping through hoops, trying desperately to insulate ourselves from all forms of pain and discomfort. In the midst of our theatrics, we don't even notice the depth, the breadth, the dimension, or the abundance of life God has for us on his paths.

While we reject the wisdom of staying on such a prescribed, narrow path, venturing out into the thickets on our own free accord in the frustratingly empty search for fulfillment, God simply says, "My paths drip with abundance."

Here's the real kicker. The freedom we frantically grope after is here. Freedom is in the furrows. Freedom is in the intimacy with God that only God's paths lead you to. Free will is not the means to the end of ultimate lack of restraint. Freedom is the result of fulfillment, which only comes through intimacy with God. Being completely naked, totally vulnerable, absolutely bell-and-whistle-less in the warm embrace of your heavenly Father is the most liberating place on earth. You can't buy it. You can't bottle it. You can't earn it. You can't do anything but move into it. That is what your free will is for.

Hopefully, we can begin to understand a different kind of freedom—a freedom that comes with a new identity. We are free because we are in Christ, not because we can make any choice we want, anytime we want. His paths are not a series of circuitous lines that meander aimlessly around your cage. The path starts at the door of your cage and blazes a trail into eternity. I can only hope and pray that the readers of this book will find the courage to take the first step onto God's pathway. Remember, as Christians we are connected to our Ground Control. Stay connected to your Ground Control. Stay on God's path and begin the journey out of the cage into abundant life.

18
DISH RAGS AND DEEP PLACES

Mary has chosen what is better, and it will not be taken away from her.

—JESUS
LUKE 10:42

Growth means change and change involves risk, stepping from the known to the unknown.

—AUTHOR UNKNOWN

It is amazing how God picks some of the most peculiar times to educate us about his character.

I was at a staff conference in the fall of 1999. It was the last hour of the third and last day. Bob Mitchell, a former president of Young Life, and his wife Claudia had joined us in our time together. Bob and Claudia were leading us in a repetitive reading of Scripture known as *Lectio Divina*.[1]

I have added the passage in Luke 10 we were reading.

As Jesus and his disciples were on their way, he came to a village where a woman named Martha opened her home to him. She had a sister called Mary, who sat at the Lord's feet listening to what he said. But Martha was distracted by all the preparations that had to be made. She came to him and asked, "Lord, don't you care that my sister has left me to do the work by myself? Tell her to help me!"

"Martha, Martha," the Lord answered, "you are worried and upset about many things, but only one thing is needed. Mary has chosen what is better, and it will not be taken away from her." [2]

As we will see in the next chapter, reading Scripture should be considered a sacred act. What I have come to love about the discipline of *Lectio Divina* is that it moves Scripture reading in a sacred direction.

However, I was a busy man.

I had been at this conference for three days. The workload back home was stacking up. The need to get home and get something done was overwhelming. I had to get out!

After the third reading of the above passage, I was hatching an escape plan. I could nonchalantly slide towards the bathroom and then make a break for my Jeep. I could be twenty miles down the road before anybody noticed I was gone.

My right foot was involuntarily tapping the floor in anticipation of making my move when I suddenly sensed the Lord saying, *Relax. Take a deep breath and listen to my words.*

This is funny on so many levels. The one that sticks out the most now, though, is how many times I've said that to my own children over the last ten years.

And then it happened. As soon as I took a deep breath and sank back in my chair, I was no longer in a staff conference. I was in the room with Martha, Mary, Jesus, and a whole bunch of other people.

You can call it an overactive imagination or a Scripture-induced hallucination. But when you can smell the cooking fire, feel the humidity from a room packed full of people and the moisture on your hands from washing dishes, it sure doesn't seem imagined.

I felt as if I had been transported to a small house in Bethany in the early first century. The house was a basic rectangle, twenty-five-ish by fifty-ish feet, with another small room off of one corner used for cooking. The floor was hard-packed dirt. The walls were grotto-like, roughly finished with stone and mortar.

I was standing in an opening where the larger room connected to the smaller kitchen area. I had an apron on. My hands were wet. I had a dishrag slung over my left shoulder. I could feel its dampness through my shirt. I was drying my hands on the dishrag while I was looking across to the opposite end of the room.

The room was packed full of people sitting on the dirt floor. It was very quiet except for the sound of Jesus' voice flowing strongly, evenly from his place across the room. He was sitting on something. What was it? I couldn't tell. I was trying to see if it was a chair, a crate, a small table, but something was in my way. It was Mary.

She sat so close to him. Her head was resting on the outside of his left thigh as she sat on the floor next to him listening. I couldn't help thinking, "is this appropriate?" She's so ... *close* to him. I searched Jesus' body language as he spoke. He was completely comfortable. Although I was situated behind most of the crowd, I ran my eyes across the faces I could see, searching for any sign of discomfort from the crowd. No one seemed to notice that this was odd. No one seemed to think twice about how Mary was so comfortable being so close to Jesus. I kept thinking, "She so near, so ..."

As my mind raced to find the word I was searching for, something washed over me that was stunning in its timing and impact.

Intimate.

That's the word I was looking for.

Fear.

That's what immediately washed over me.

Bam! There I was back in a staff conference. No aroma of cooking fires, dust, and sweaty people; just the soft, spoken words of Scripture flowing steadily from Bob Mitchell.

The violence of the realization was shocking. It hit me with such force it propelled me right out of this "experience" straight back into the real world of staff conferences and to-do lists.

Needless to say, I was confused and extremely concerned by the message of my *Lectio Divina* experience. After all, I was a Christian. In fact I had been a Christian for over twenty years. How on earth can this be right?

How can I be afraid of intimacy with God?

Maybe I wasn't afraid of "do-your-quiet-time-be-a-good-Christian" intimacy. I knew, though, that I was extremely afraid of the kind of intimacy I saw during my "experience."

In a single moment I was forced to begin reconciling a few facts I had come to believe with a few realities that were completely at odds with those facts. The first fact that came under fire was the "God is much more interested in what I can do for him than anything else" fact.

"If that's not a fact," I believed, "then what is the Great Commission for?" Moreover, how can I grade myself as a Christian without some goals, some markers, some qualifiers on how I'm doing as a follower of Christ? In my deep heart I truly believed, "Sure, God *loves* everybody. But let's be honest, he only *likes* the ones that are on the team, the ones who are making it happen on the field. He's the Great Coach of the Universe that only *likes* you when you are scoring points for his team. I'm sure God loves the bench-warmers but he really digs the marquee players."

What I really thought was, "God can't love me alone. There's just not much here without my Christian activity or accomplishments. Even if I don't get much done, God will like me better just because of my 'never-say-die' attitude."

What Jesus confronted me with in the home of Martha and Mary is that my activity for God was ill-conceived. It was actually counter-productive. My focus was on what I should be doing for him when he only wants one thing:

"Mary has chosen what is better."

Suddenly my head became very crowded. Everyone—the shadowy impostor, the serious competitor, the competent achiever, the go-to-guy, the slimy faker—were all screaming in rebellion, "But she's *sitting* on the floor! She's not *doing* anything!"

I felt betrayed. How could this be?

God has to be more interested in …

God has to be more interested in his kingdom …

God has to be more interested in himself than …

… in me …

It was news to me that God is way more interested in me than in himself. Let that sink in. God is always more interested in you than in what you can do for him.

Jesus is clear: "Martha has chosen what is better and it will not be taken away from her."

Unfortunately, our cage mentality tells us that we will have nothing if we stop the performance. We feel as if we will slide off the face of the planet if we are not doing something for God. I felt as if a black hole would swallow me up if my planner wasn't full, my phone wasn't ringing, or ministry wasn't growing.

There are many things I could do to "suffer for Jesus" but *sitting* wasn't one of them. Why couldn't it be "executing a well-orchestrated plan at the feet of Jesus?" or "knocking it out of the park at the feet of Jesus?" or "working at the feet of Jesus?" But *sitting*? Really?

In contrast to Martha's git-r-done attitude that we Americans admire so much, Mary's inactivity seems downright unproductive, lazy, and irresponsible. In context of this passage it does indeed seem unusual.

If the president of the United States were coming to have dinner at my house—I'd remodel. OK, I wouldn't remodel, but I'd probably re-paint ... *everything*. OK, maybe I wouldn't re-paint everything, but everywhere he would be in the house. Then I'd make sure that the carpet was clean, the windows were spotless, the blinds were ... trash the blinds and get new ones! The moldy stuff around the vent covers would be dealt with. All dust bunnies and little cobwebby things in the corner of the family room would be swept away. The yard would be immaculate and the food amazing.

I, for one, feel Martha's pain. It's not the president of the United States who is coming to dinner, it's the President of the Entire Universe who is coming to dinner. When we think about serving God, there is no more immediate, visceral, practical way to serve God than to feed him ... while he's sitting in the living room!

Martha was tweaked! I would be too! But God in the flesh says something amazing. He says, "*Martha, Martha, you are worried and upset by many things* (i.e., dirty blinds, chipped paint, dust bunnies, cobwebby things, etc.) *but only one thing is needed...*"

In the time since my *Lectio Divina* experience, I have learned that sitting is a beautiful thing. Even more than that, though, sitting at the feet of Jesus is the single most life-giving thing we can do as human beings.

Scratching and clawing while being dragged against the very grain of my being, I have learned that *doing* gets in the way of *being*. I'm not saying love is inaction or faith is sedentary acquiescence to circumstances. I am saying that much of our "work for God" is misguided busyness that hinders true intimacy with the father heart of God.

There. I said it.

We spend inordinate amounts of time and energy working on seeing "fruit" in our lives. In the process of being focused on the fruit, we forget about the roots. Fruit is great, but life, freedom, fulfillment, meaning, and direction will not come from fruit. Those things will only come through careful consideration, investment, and cultivation of the roots. The roots bring nourishment and life to the plant so fruit can be produced. We cannot produce one more apple, orange, or peach by trying to produce one more apple, orange, or peach. Copious amounts of fruit will naturally follow when we devote our resources to the roots.

Unfortunately, as a Christian culture we are enamored with fruit. Statistics show us again and again that the primary way we measure our faith is based on lifestyle.[3] In grading ourselves on a moral bell curve, we have traded *being* for *doing*. When we are living this reality it is no longer Christianity. It is moralism.[4] It seems we are borderline pathological when it comes to doing "good things" and not doing "bad things." So much so that those on the outside of Christianity define us by this very behavior. Is this what life in Christ is all about? Is this the message of the cross? Is this the overarching desire of the father heart of God? Is this the purpose of the torn veil?

Am I advocating libertine Christianity? Am I dismissing

"godly living"? Absolutely not, but at some point we are going to have to realize that the cart has been before the horse for a very long time. Intimacy with God will bring Christ-likeness. Trying to conform to somebody's idea of Christ-likeness will only bring confusion, frustration, emptiness, and death. In short, trying to be Christ-like will not bring intimacy with God.

The great lesson of the parable of the sower[5] is this: The soil needs to be changed. The human heart has to be changed. Only God can accomplish this through our faith in the redemptive blood of Christ. Roots grow in the heart of flesh God has given us, but we still act as if we have hearts of stone[6] when we devote our resources to what is visible on the outside. We continue to believe our worth is in our performance. We believe our value is found in how good we can get our tree to look. While we focus on the fruit, the roots wither in the new soil of our redeemed hearts. Our need to *do* gets in the way of God's desire for us to *be*.

The question is not, "What are you going to *do* to find fulfillment, intimacy, or direction in life?" The question is, "What are you going to *be*?" Being with Jesus will lead to doing for God. Doing for God seldom, if ever, leads to being with Jesus.[7]

Together, we have assessed many things in the pages of this book. We have thought about fleas and sandboats, tree forts and cages, fear and control, process and performance, freedom, free will, and fulfillment. Together, we have considered the very essence of life itself. The many things we have evaluated together in these pages have brought us to one great question: What is the goal? What is the purpose of the Christian life? Is it to be Christ-like? Is it to be agents of kingdom-change in the world? Is it to be Jesus to a broken world? Is it to bring glory to God in word and deed?

Remember my friend Matt from chapter 6? His full name was Matthew Ryan Beveridge. Matt was diagnosed with mononucleosis and then cat scratch fever before his cancer was discovered. After a two-year struggle with cancer, Matt went to be with Jesus on Friday, October 10, 2008. He was only twenty years old, yet his closeness to Jesus might be one of the most beautiful things I have ever seen.

Even as Matt was dying, he was full of life. He was full of life because he lived his life intimately connected to his source. Matt focused on the roots, not the fruit. He counted his sickness as a blessing because it moved him into deeper places of trust and depth with Jesus. Through two years of tests, surgeries, and chemotherapies, no one ever heard Matt complain, whine, or ask, "Why me?" No one heard it because Matt never said it.

The day before his first chemo treatment, Matt and I were sitting in the Alkek Lobby of the M.D. Anderson Cancer Center in Houston. We were eating pizza and talking about nothing in particular when I asked him, "Have you thought about where this thing could go?" The reply from the then-seventeen-year-old was staggering. He thought for a second and said, "I don't want to be sick. I don't want to have to go through this but I'm OK if God uses this to draw people to him. To live is Christ. To die is gain."

Watching my mother die from cancer just a few years before only eight floors above the very spot I was sitting, I thought, "He's young. He has no idea what could be ahead of him."

As it played out, though, I was continually amazed at how Matt lived out his days. He was completely unfazed. It wasn't because Matt didn't care or was unaware of his circumstances. It was because Matt was intimately connected to Jesus. That fact became more and more apparent to everyone who was attached to his story. In the end, for Matt, dying was just a formality. He was already so close to Jesus that dying was the only way to close the only distance that remained.

I don't know about you, but when I die, I want to die like that. In the end, Matt didn't teach me how to die. He taught me how to live even more deeply connected to my source.

That, in the end, is the purpose of the Christian life: living deeply connected to Jesus. Intimacy with God will bring Christ-likeness. Intimacy with God will bring action in the face of injustice and suffering. Intimacy with God will bring glory to God. Intimacy with God will bring light in dark places.[8] It will build a thousand cities on a thousand hills.[9]

Sitting at the feet of Jesus is the only thing that is needed. Mary has chosen what is better and it will not be taken away from her. Don't settle for second best. Don't settle for *doing* when you were made for *being*. Do your soul a favor and do some world class sitting at the feet of Jesus today!

19
CONVERGENCE

Convergence: a coming together from different directions.

—MERRIAM-WEBSTER DICTIONARY

Life is a highway.
I want to ride it all night long.

—RASCAL FLATTS
"ME AND MY GANG"

Any discussion about moving out of the cage will need to include some thoughts on God's will. Some will say quite plainly that if we "hear" God in any way other than through Scripture, we are in error. You will have to decide for yourself: Is God the Holy Spirit, who lives in us, mute? Regardless of where you land on this question, there are some things to consider when considering God's will for your life.

One thing that will derail any search for truth in your life is insincerity. If you are not absolutely, totally, and honestly sincere, do not even begin the process. If you are not ready to hear what God has to say, take some more laps until you are ready. Do not approach this question until you are ready to hear what he has to say.

The baseline for knowing God's will for your life starts with believing God *has* a will for your life. I know that sounds like a ridiculous thing to say. However, many Christians bump along not altogether convinced that God really has much to say about their day-to-day lives.

Once again: swing and a miss.

The father heart of God desires to be intimately involved in your life. You could read the Jewish dietary laws in Leviticus and come away feeling like God is a serious control freak. On the other hand, you could see those same passages as being reflective of a God who is very interested in all aspects of our lives.

Since you have made it this far in this book I hope you have picked up a sense of the latter—God is interested in the details. We're the ones with the fear of rejection, and control and trust issues.

Many Christians' prayer lives consist of the "Big Three" and a lot of Hail Mary's. I don't mean the "hail Mary full of grace" prayer either. I mean the clock-is-running-out-and-you-need-God-to-save-you Hail Mary prayers. You know the kind: The final exam you didn't study for, the boss doesn't come back in town today, turbulence on the airplane prayers. The "Big Three" revolve loosely around, "Is this the school I should go to? Is this the job I should take? Is this the person I should marry?" Mixing these together or praying them over and over is not a recipe for intimacy. The inability to sense God's direction, in many cases, is symptomatic of a non-existent prayer life.[1] Out of that lack of intimacy comes a skewed perspective on knowing God's will.

God's will can be known. More directly, God's will for your life can be known *by you*. The Bible is full of wonderful accounts of how God has revealed himself. He has and continues to reveal himself even now. One of the best known is in the first chapter of Romans.

> For since the creation of the world God's invisible qualities—his eternal power and divine nature— have been clearly seen, being understood from what has been made, so that men are without excuse.[2]

In *The Knowledge of the Holy*, A. W. Tozer writes of an incomprehensible God:

> The effort of inspired men to express the ineffable has placed a great strain upon both thought and language in the Holy Scriptures. These being often a revelation of a world above nature, and the minds for which they were written being a part of nature, the writers are compelled to use a great many 'like' words to make themselves understood.[3]

God is incomprehensible. Being incomprehensible, however, does not make him unknowable. Inhabiting a world "above nature" does not preclude God from also inhabiting nature. An incomprehensible God can and has chosen to make himself known.

The veil is torn. God is not hiding. His fingerprints are all over the last sunset you saw. His majesty is in the snow-capped Rocky Mountains. His power is in the waves that crash upon the shoreline. His infinite creative ability is literally in the stars. He is visible and knowable in a very experiential, natural sense.

As he reveals himself in nature, he has also revealed himself in Scripture. Reading Scripture is not limited to a physical reading and comprehension of words on a page. God has revealed himself in Scripture because he *is* Scripture. John 1:14 states, "The Word became flesh." Simply stated: Scripture is Jesus. When you read Scripture you are communing with Christ in a very intimate way. You are partaking of the living Word of God. In a perfect world, reading Scripture would be sacramental.

God revealing himself in nature is awesome. Revealing himself in Scripture is amazing. But for an intimate, relational God, that wasn't good enough. He made it personal. He revealed himself to us as *us*. The incarnation is an extremely intimate event in its transparency. We actually get to see what God is like. Unlike us, with our smoke and mirrors and bobbing and weaving, God comes straight out and says, "Here I am."

Tozer goes on to say:

> As Deep calleth unto deep, and though polluted and land-locked by the mighty disaster theologians call the Fall, the soul senses its origin and longs to return to its Source. How can this be realized? The answer of the Bible is simply "through Jesus Christ our Lord." In Christ and by Christ, God effects complete self-disclosure ...[4]

How does God feel about hypocrisy? How does God feel about you and me? How does God deal with awkward situations? It's all there. I'm not saying it. Jesus said it: "You see me, you see God."[5]

God has revealed and is revealing himself in nature, in Scripture, and in Christ. He is visible and knowable.

Now that we have poured a foundation, let's dispel a few misconceptions about knowing God's will. The first misconception would be: "When God shows me his will for my life, I will see it in one all-life-encompassing-vision that will make complete sense to me."

That would be another strike.

That's just not the character of God. He is not going to manhandle you to the ground and force-feed you his will for your entire life in one sitting. The father heart of God is more interested in your pressing into him. That's why he whispers.

Elijah was on a mountain top.[6] Scripture says a great fire came, but there was no word from God in the fire. A great earthquake came, but there was no word from God in the earthquake either. But then the voice of God came in a whisper. A whisper. How beautifully intimate is that? Like a lover. Like I would hold my children close when they were babies and whisper "Sweet dreams" into their ear at bedtime.

His will won't be in the thunder. It won't be in a loud display of wonder that blows you away. It will be soft. It will be intimate. It will be a whisper.

There is another reason God will not transport you to the nearest mountain top and show you your divine purpose in one glorious panoramic view. Remember Kramer from *Seinfeld*? This will not happen simply because you will "Kramer." "I'm flippin' out here, Jerry!" If you could even grasp it, you would tank under the overwhelming specter of this alternate universe. There is no way our finite minds could comprehend our lives twenty years down the road with God.

Accordingly, God will give you the tip of his will. It's digestible. It's somewhat easier to comprehend. You can get your hands around it. This, however, leads us to the next misconception: "I'm going to like God's will for my life."

I mean he knows the desires of your heart, right? Surely he will blend all your acquired skills, natural abilities, and spiritual gifts into one sweet package deal, right?

Yes.

But that still doesn't mean you're going to like it. The words we use such as "like" and "love" really don't belong in a discussion about discerning God's will. Searching out and entering into God's will for your life is about pursuing intimacy with God. When you walk with Jesus intimately, the sweet journey of life unfolds before you. When intimacy is your goal, other concerns fade away.

Once you have arrived at a place where you believe God does reveal himself to us and his will can be known for your life, there are a few things to consider.

First, since God has revealed himself in Scripture, that would be a good place to start. Christians are notorious for saying, "Oh yeah, it's God's Word, praise Jesus!" But how many times do we pick it up? If we really believe the Bible is the living Word of God, it probably wouldn't gather quite so much dust.

I've been there, though. In college I renamed my bed, "the Word." Then when someone called and asked what I was doing, I could say, "I'm just getting some time in the Word."

Give me a break. I was in college!

I've been in discussions with many Christians over the age of twenty-two who are seeking God's direction for their lives. I believe most were sincere in their quest. Unfortunately, many had not picked up a Bible in a very long time. The day you want to know God's will for your life is not the day to start reading the Bible! Start reading the Bible *now* and decisions you make in the future will be rooted in Scripture. Whether you started reading today or twenty years ago, the non-negotiable remains: Your decisions in life should be bathed in prayerful reading of Scripture.

After searching the Scripture, another step in the process of discerning God's will is this: wise counsel. Let's get something straight about wise counsel. Wise counsel is different from advice. I do my best to let people know that there is a difference between my wise counsel and my advice.

Wise counsel should be absolutely rooted in Scripture. Advice is rooted in personal experience. Advice from three different people may well be all over the map. Experience has shown me that wise counsel from a number of different people points in the same direction.

Most often, wise counsel will come from someone

who is further down the road in their walk with Christ than you are. Their life should be reflective of someone who walks with Jesus. Their trustworthiness and confidentiality should be unquestionable.

Wise counsel is of great value. We should never underestimate what God is doing through our brothers and sisters in Christ. Decisions in life—especially big decisions—should be made in community. There is safety in the "multitude of counsel."[7] The Bible exhorts us to seek counsel. I don't pretend to know all the reasons why Scripture encourages us to seek counsel, but I sure know one: I don't have the corner on truth. Neither do you.

We have this idea that truth and error live on polar opposites of the decision curve. They don't. Truth and error live next door. Since you and I don't own the truth, we should adhere to the clear biblical directive: Seek wise counsel. There is safety in the multitude of counsel.

Let me repeat the necessity for absolute sincerity in this process. It may sound ridiculous, but if you seek wise counsel and it is pointing a direction: Go that direction!

Yes. It has been done: People, myself included, have actually gone the *opposite* direction of the wise counsel they have sought. (I try to block these blunders out of my memory, but to no avail.) There have been times in my life when I knew the direction I was supposed to go and, yes, went another direction entirely. Predictably, the results were ooooooooogly (that means really, really ugly.) Unfortunately, I have also been privileged to offer wise counsel and then watch the recipients of said wise counsel go their own way.

Yep. Oooooogly. Sincerity is critical.

As you are prayerfully considering God's word, you are looking for places that are merging with the wise counsel you have sought. As you are looking for merging points, you should be aware of what is right around you.

You should be aware of the circumstances in your life because God is God, and, as we saw in chapter 11 he has purposed to work in partnership with you beginning with where you are this very instance. Regardless of the poor decisions you have made in life or the "mistakes" you have made, don't be misled. God has not been caught off guard. He is not looking down at the jagged path of your life and just now exclaiming, "Oh, me! How did this happen?"

Prayerfully considering your immediate circumstances, along with seeking wise counsel while being in the Word, you will begin to see convergence. Convergence is a crazy thing. Only God can pull it off. Convergence will help you know it is him.

Before we look further at knowing the will of God, let me say this about the "process" of discerning God's will. First, remember the secret of the tree fort? God is much more interested in the process than the product. We are interested in results. We run around doing all sorts of stuff and then stop and ask God, "Don't you like it? I made it just for you!" Again, God is not disappointed in you for the effort. That's not how he desires to live life with you, though.

The "process" of knowing God's will really isn't a

process. It is a result. Knowing God's will is a result of living life with God in a wonderful, intimate, adventurous journey. When you approach Scripture, prayer, and the community of Christ with an eternal perspective, you come to look at decisions from the inside looking out, instead of the outside looking in. When you walk in step with the very heartbeat of God, you are dealing with the ultimate in inside information.

There are a few more things to consider when discerning God's will for your life.

First, the will of God is highly subjective. There are the scriptural boundaries that objectively express certain things as out of bounds. For instance, if you were looking at this great new job that entailed robbing drug dealers and giving the proceeds to the poor, you would be outside—*way* outside—the expressed, objective will of God.

Beyond the objective directives we are given in God's Word, his will for your life is quite a subjective affair. God did not tattoo "Father of Many Nations" across Abram's forehead for the world to see. Essentially, God came to Abram and said, "Abram, I know this land of Ur has been home to you, your father, and your father's father. I'm sure you are very comfortable here, and I know you're kind of a 'big deal' around these parts, but I want you to get your goats and cows and stuff and hit the road."

Go. Just pack a bag and hit the road. No external, visible, objective sign of any kind. God showed him the tip of his will and Abraham believed God. Abraham moved out of his cage and the rest is history.

The tip of God's will for your life is not hidden. If you have been honest with God and yourself and have come to see that you are still in your cage, the tip of God's will is right in there with you. It will take moving out of your cage to live it. It is a guarantee that if you follow it, though, you will move out of your cage.

The second thing you should know about God's will is: Obedience is better than sacrifice.

God was crystal clear with King Saul.[8] Saul was to destroy the Amalekites. He was not to let one living thing survive. Saul knew God's will, but blatantly disregarded it by keeping the best animals alive.

The prophet Samuel came to confront Saul on his disobedience. Saul's reply is painful to hear. Not because I feel *his* pain, but because I feel my own. How many times have I absolutely known what God was leading me to and I completely disregarded it? Too many.

Maybe you have felt that pain too. It is a bitter pill to swallow. It is hard enough to admit to ourselves, much less to God, that we just decided to go another way.

Saul's response to Samuel is so uncomfortably lame you can almost hear the thud of hollow words as they come out of his mouth and drop awkwardly to the floor, "Well," ... thud! ... "I kept them" ... thud! ... "so we could" ... thud! ... "sacrifice them" ... thud! ... "to God" ... double thud!

Ouch. I would not want to have been anywhere near there at that moment. The level of discomfort is palpable. It is so intense I almost have to turn away just reading about it.

What is harder to comprehend is what Samuel drives home to Saul: Obedience is better than sacrifice.

We have seen that when we move through life in step with God, life is what he intended it to be. When we move through life out of step with God, we miss out on all the goodness, blessing, satisfaction, and fulfillment God has for us. As Samuel so clearly illustrated to Saul, when it's gone it's gone, and there is no amount of sacrifice that will bring it back.

We never get back through sacrifice what we lose through disobedience to God. As we saw in chapter 17, obedience is abundance. Being in God's furrows brings the abundance of the harvest. Deciding to go another way brings disappointment and frustration.

There is another thing to know about the will of God: it may be counterintuitive. After you have stacked up all the pros and cons, the revealed will of God may run in complete opposition to what you and others may consider to be a rational choice.

We see this very often. A common example is the "church search." A family will come into church, look around and leave. When the director of assimilation follows up with them to see if they found a church home, they will say that said church didn't have the right worship, right preaching, right number of children, was too big, too small, too boring, or too rowdy.

That is a cage mentality. It doesn't cross our minds that God could possibly be calling us to a church so we can serve, teach, lead, or learn from that particular expression of the body of Christ! It's inconceivable to us that God might call us to a certain place because we need to be submitted to spiritual authority in that church. No. Instead we do the cost/benefit analysis and go with the most logical choice.

Finally, many Christians consider the "open door" policy in discerning God's will for their lives (as in, "God opened the door, so I took went through it"). This is generally accepted as a wise way to discern God's intentions.

Generally, I would agree. The first thing to consider with this approach, though, is that the door to where you are now should be closed or closing in the foreseeable future. Too many times this method of discerning God's will is only a cover up for a "grass is greener" situation. We don't like something that is happening where we are so we start looking for other open doors. My first question to someone asking for wise counsel on an open door in their life will never have to do with the open door. It will have to do with what is going on in their life at the moment.

Of course, this is not always the case. God could be moving you from one place to another without closing doors.

Also, contrary to popular belief, there are no "unanswered prayers." God always answers prayers. He does not give us the silent treatment. The problem is that we only want to hear one answer: "Yes." That unfortunately is only one of three possible answers. The other two are, "No" and "Wait."

We don't like those much.

Therein a problem arises with the "open door" policy.

The door may be open, but it doesn't mean we are to step through it. God could be saying, "Wait." Let's face it. We are not the picture of patience and long suffering. When faced with "wait," open doors tend to turn into black holes that suck us toward them with seemingly irresistible power.

This is why prayerful consideration of God's word along with God's people in the midst of the God-ordained circumstances in your life is a process you can only benefit from.

Of course, we now know that the "process" is really intended to bring us into deeper intimacy with God. If, on the way to discovering God's will for our lives, intimacy with God is an imposition, maybe other questions should be asked first.

In the end, as Christians, we have redeemed hearts and a God who is not going to let us mess up our lives. Is your heart turned towards God? Can you lay your head on your pillow at night and say, "Today I did my level best to follow God"?

The unholy trinity is powerless against a will that is set towards intimacy with God. Do you love God? Follow God out of the cage. His sheep hear his voice.[9] Reject anything you know is not God[10] and move out. Many think that following God is a long, arduous road with a thousand intersections and a thousand red lights.

Go. Stop. Go. Stop. Go. Stop.

Quite the contrary. God's will is an open highway through the most beautiful country you could ever imagine. Yes, you will have to pull over every once in awhile to check the map, fuel up, and get some munchies. Other than that, though, pull the top down, feel the wind in your hair, and take the ride of your life.

That was the lecture. Here's the lab: Stop reading about it and go do it! The only way that is going to happen is if you move out of your cage. Anything you may "hear" from God is an untested hypothesis in the cage. It must be tested in the laboratory of life outside the cage. The lecture is in the cage. The lab is out there. Go and meet God. He's standing at the door.

20

SAIL ON

… on a wind whose breath will deliver me from the blackened path to the turquoise sea and beyond.

—BILLY CERVENY

"SAIL ON"

Jesus is lore.

—FLIGHTPATH COFFEEHOUSE

AUSTIN, TEXAS

My definition of success is never saying "no" to Jesus.

—MOTHER TERESA

I grew up watching Saturday morning cartoons. One of my favorite cartoons was Casper the Friendly Ghost. Casper would always want to make friends with the living, but it never seemed to work out too well. Every time someone saw Casper, their eyes would bulge out of their heads, and they would scream, "It's a g-g-g-g-g-g-ghost!" Casper would slink sadly away only to return to save the day by the end of the cartoon.

When it comes to the reality of Jesus Christ in the twenty-first century, a rapidly secularizing world views

179

Christ as not much more than a mythic figure. An apparition. A ghost.

A wooden fence runs along the patio outside the Flightpath Coffeehouse in Austin, Texas. On this fence is a carving that says, "Jesus is lore."

Admittedly, it is a clever play on "Jesus is Lord." It is interesting, though, that "Jesus is lore" is a carving. Obviously, someone was very intent on letting the world know that Jesus is not real. He is made up, fictional, lore. He is a ghost.

There are a number of reasons we should move out of our cages. First, we have seen that it is simply the way God desires to live in intimate partnership with us. Second, outside the cage is where we will find ourselves. There is no self-help system, pop psychology plan, or misguided notion of self-sufficiency that will substitute for finding your purpose in the deep, father heart of God.

Lastly, Jesus is not a ghost. When Peter stepped out of that boat and walked on water, he proved something to everyone in the boat who was crying, "It's a ghost!" He proved that Jesus was real. He was flesh and blood. He was not an apparition. He was not a ghost.

This is one of the most important things that will happen when Christians get out of their cages. They will prove that Jesus is real. He is alive. He is not lore, but the living Son of God. God knows this dark world is dying to know a living Lord. As long as we stay in our cages, though, Jesus will continue to become more and more of a legend that people only talk about in churches.

We started this journey with a few fleas in a jar. We have seen that we are all born in a cage. As Christians, Jesus has unlocked that door, swung it open, and said, "Come, follow me!" Many of us have opted to stay put. The door to the cage might as well still be locked. We have voluntarily accepted captivity. Functionally, the voluntary acceptance of captivity is slavery. A great evil has been committed because our identity as noble, valuable, free, redeemed children of God is diminished when we accept slavery instead of freedom.

In *The Art of War*, Sun Tzu writes:

> So it is said that if you know others and know yourself, you will not be imperiled in a hundred battles; if you do not know others but know yourself, you win one and lose one; if you do not know others and do not know yourself, you will be imperiled in every single battle.[1]

Most will remember Sun Tzu for the rough translation of "Know your enemy." As seen in the full quote above, however, equally important in Sun Tzu's mind was knowing yourself. You cannot know yourself if you are not honest with yourself.

My great hope is that we as Christians become honest with ourselves. Are you in your cage? If you are, be honest about it. Engage that incredible engine God gave you called free will and move out of your cage.

Is it messy? Yes! Will you need help? Absolutely! Will you look foolish? Probably! Will you lose money? Maybe. Will you be comfortable? Not at first, but you get used to it! Will you experience failure if you venture out of your cage? More than likely! Will you succeed? Yes, but who cares?!

Living outside the cage is not about success and failure. It is about faithfulness.

I saw an interview once with Mother Teresa. The interviewer listed off some of the amazing things this woman of God had done. He then asked the diminutive, fragile little nun what made her so successful.

Her answer marked me for life. She simply said, "Never saying 'no' to Jesus."

In her own way, Mother Teresa was telling us the Christian life is not about success and failure. It is about faithfulness. It is about never saying "no" to Jesus. This may be the single greatest reason why you will experience true freedom outside the cage. Outside the cage the arbitrary, man-made constructs of success and failure do not apply. What matters outside the cage is simply saying "yes" to the father heart of God.

You will learn to trust God in ways that may be unimaginable to you now. The more you say, "yes" to Jesus, the further and further he will lead you out until your cage is a distant memory.

That, more than anything, may define Christian growth best of all. Will you grow in intimacy with God? Absolutely! Will you experience the true freedom that only comes from moving out of your cage? Yes. Yes. Yes.

I believe you will experience a soul-gratifying freedom that far surpasses mere absence of restraint because you have reclaimed your identity. You are a beautiful, majestic sailboat born to grace this life with only the wood, canvas, and paint your Master Builder lovingly and meticulously handcrafted.

Staying in your cage doesn't make you any less saved. It doesn't make you any less appealing or loved by God.

Moving out of the cage is not hard. It's simple. Christianity was not designed to operate inside the cage. Jesus is standing at the door. Will you say, "yes" to him right now?

> He spake with Abraham at the oak,
> He called Elisha from the plough;
> David he from the sheepfolds took,
> Thy day, thine hour of grace, is now.[2]

When the angel of God came to Gideon to tell him what God had in store for him, Gideon came up with a whole bunch of excuses. After his whining and complaining had obviously fallen on deaf ears, Gideon heard these words:

> "The Lord is with you, mighty warrior … Go in the strength you have"[3]

Your cage is your tomb. It is the place where you died to you, your dreams, and ambitions, your will for your life, your desires. It is the final resting place of the poser, faker, and the impostor. The stone has been rolled away. The door has swung wide open for you to walk out in the resurrected, *zoe*[4] life that God has placed in all those who believe. The same power that worked in the tomb of

Christ our Savior is the same power that lives inside you.

The faith that unlocked your cage is the same faith that will lead you out of your cage. You don't need a seminary degree. You don't need a specialized set of skills. You don't even need the clothes on your back. You already have everything you need. Go in the strength you have. God will do the rest.

> By entering through faith into what God has always wanted to do for us—set us right with him, make us fit for him—we have it all together with God because of our Master Jesus. And that's not all: We throw open our doors to God and discover at the same moment that he has already thrown open his door to us. We find ourselves standing where we always hoped we might stand—out in the wide open spaces of God's grace and glory, standing tall and shouting our praise.[5]

On this day, may you be known and loved in the deep, father heart of God. May you begin to rediscover your true identity as a redeemed one of God.

Sail on, my brothers and sisters in Christ!

ACKNOWLEDGMENTS

To my God, who has fathered me with his passionate, pursuing love.

To my wife, Shawna, who is and has always been Jesus to me. Thank you for knowing me … and still loving me so well.

To my kids: Colton, Mikaela and Carson. You have shown me God's love is wider, deeper, and longer than I could have ever imagined.

To Koby, Chris, Pete, and Bobby. You are more than friends. You are my band of brothers in Christ.

To every Young Life leader who has ever shown up on a campus to love kids the way you find them. You are "proof of life." Never stop telling them about Jesus!

To all of those who responded to my pleas for help in the cite work for this book. To Kari Kurz for pulling Psalm 65 out of the obscurity of the "outtakes," Hank Nuss, Dr. Clay Butler, Dr. David Lewis, Wade Grassedonio, the C. S. Lewis Society, and The Abraham Lincoln Association.

Posthumously to Dr. Harold Hoehner, Distinguished Professor of New Testament Studies, Dallas Theological Seminary. A man who had forgotten more about the life of Paul than I will probably ever know. I'm grateful for his lesson that academics don't always come at the expense of passion.

NOTES

Unless otherwise noted, all verses are from the New International Version, and all emphasis is the author's.

CHAPTER ONE: SANDBOAT

1. The flea facts are from http://www.nofleas.com/ Flea-Facts.asp.
2. Ephesians 1:3–4 (The Message)

CHAPTER TWO: BITTERSWEET SYMPHONY

1. Primo Levi, *The Drowned and the Saved* (Random House, New York, New York, 1989), pp. 125–126.

CHAPTER THREE: HEART OF THE MATTER

1. Matthew 4:3
2. John 1:10
3. John 3:16
4. 1 John 2:15
5. 2 Corinthians 10:3–5
6. Ezekiel 11:19
7. 2 Corinthians 5:17
8. John 1:1; 20:28; Hebrews 1:8; Romans 9:5; 2 Peter 1:1; 1 John 5:20
9. Isaiah 9:6
10. Matthew 1:23
11. Revelation 1:8; 22:13

12. John 6:35; 6:48
13. 1 John 2:22
14. John 1:3; Colossians 1:16
15. Revelation 19:13
16. John 1:9
17. Acts 7:52; 1 John 2:1
18. Zephaniah 3:17
19. Psalm 56:8
20. 2 Corinthians 5:21
21. Revelation 19:6–8
22. Hosea 11:8 (KJV)

CHAPTER FOUR: TALK TO THE HAND

1. Brennan Manning, *The Rabbi's Heartbeat* (NavPress, Colorado Springs, Colorado, 2003), preface to chapter 1.
2. Ibid., p. 14.
3. Genesis 3:8
4. Genesis 1:31
5. Ephesians 3:20
6. Romans 8:29

CHAPTER FIVE: ALLEGORY OF THE CAGE

1. Benjamin Jowett, *Allegory of the Cave* (Vintage Books, New York, New York, 1991), pp. 253–261.
2. John 18:33–38a

CHAPTER SIX: THE CAGE

1. Romans 5:8 (New American Standard Bible)
2. E. M. Bounds, *The Complete Works of E. M. Bounds on*

Prayer (Baker Books, Grand Rapids, Michigan, 1990), p. 24.

3. James 2:19

4. John 8:36 (New King James Version)

5. David Kinnaman, *unChristian* (Baker Books, Grand Rapids, Michigan, 2007), p. 47.

6. U2, "I Still Haven't Found What I'm Looking For," *The Joshua Tree*, 1987.

7. John 14:6

CHAPTER SEVEN: TOMDOSS

1. Matthew 6:33 (KJV)

2. Galatians 5:1

3. Abraham Lincoln, speaking to a crowd in Baltimore, Maryland, April 18, 1864.

CHAPTER EIGHT: DON'T ROCK THE BOAT

1. Henri Nouwen, *In the Name of Jesus: Reflections on Christian Leadership* (The Crossroad Publishing Company, New York, New York, 1989), pp. 42–43.

2. Robert Coleman, *The Master Plan of Evangelism* (Revell, Grand Rapids, Michigan, 1963), p. 24.

3. Mark 6:48

4. Matthew 14:28

CHAPTER TEN: THE TORN VEIL

1. Psalm 42:7 (KJV)

2. Matthew 27:50–51 (NKJV)

3. James 2:13

4. Romans 10:9–10

5. The Westminster Shorter Catechism.

6. William Willimon, "Powerpoint Preaching," *Leadership*, Summer 2007, p. 34.

7. Henri Nouwen, *In the Name of Jesus: Reflections on Christian Leadership* (The Crossroad Publishing Company, New York, New York, 1989), p. 10.

8. Ibid., p. 16

9. 2 Timothy 1:7 (KJV)

10. Ibid.

CHAPTER TWELVE: RULES OF LIFE

1. 1 Corinthians 2:2–4

2. 2 Corinthians 9:8

3. Romans 6:23

4. Mark 10: 17–22

5. Henri Nouwen, *In the Name of Jesus: Reflections on Christian Leadership* (The Crossroad Publishing Company, New York, New York, 1989), p. 17

6. *Encarta World English Dictionary*, Microsoft Corporation, 1999.

7. Ibid.

8. 1 Corinthians 1:25

CHAPTER THIRTEEN: PERSPECTIVE

1. This quote is widely attributed to C. S. Lewis.

2. Hebrews 11:1

CHAPTER FOURTEEN: RECONCILIATION

1. 2 Corinthians 5:17–19

CHAPTER FIFTEEN: MEAT'S IN THE STREET

1. 1 Corinthians 3:2
2. Matthew 22:34–40
3. Colossians 1:28 (The Message)
4. Matthew 14:23
5. Mark 1:35
6. Luke 6:12
7. Luke 5:16
8. Matthew 26:36

CHAPTER SIXTEEN: GROUND CONTROL TO MAJOR TOM

1. Hebrews 11:40
2. C. S. Lewis, *The Great Divorce* (Harper Collins, New York, New York, 1946).
3. Proverbs 14:12

CHAPTER SEVENTEEN: MA'GAL

1. Psalm 65:9–13 (NKJV)
2. Song of Solomon 2:4
3. Jeremiah 29:11
4. Thanks to my friend and pastor, Dr. David Lewis, for his contribution and direction on the etymology of this passage in Hebrew.
5. Jesus, John 10:10 (NKJV)

CHAPTER EIGHTEEN: DISH RAGS AND DEEP PLACES

1. *Lectio Divina* is Latin for divine or holy reading. It is a traditional monastic practice of prayer and scriptural reading intended to facilitate communion with God and to increase in the knowledge of God's Word. I highly recommend the practice.

2. Luke 10:38–42

3. David Kinnaman, *unChristian* (Baker Books, Grand Rapids, Michigan, 2007), p. 51.

4. Moralism—This is a term used to describe the act of subjectively ranking people along a linear spectrum. On one end of the spectrum is someone of superior moral virtue (i.e., Gandhi, Mother Teresa, etc.). At the other end of the spectrum is someone of great moral delinquency (Hitler, Charles Manson, etc.). When we "moralize" we place ourselves and others somewhere along this spectrum. Quite often we are placing ourselves somewhere on this scale of "good and evil" in order to ease our consciences about where we stand with God. Our hope is that at the end of our life we will have moved sufficiently far enough to the "good" end of the spectrum that God will let us into heaven. Unfortunately, none of this is in the Bible. Moralism is a man made belief system that has no relevance to biblical Christianity.

5. Matthew 13:1–23

6. Ezekiel 11:19

7. This statement is true in the context of a life that is lived in the shadow of legalism and performance. From this position, doing things for God is not going to bring intimacy with God. Doing things in partnership with God in a pre-ordained purpose for your life will bring intimacy.

8. Matthew 5:14

9. Ibid.

CHAPTER NINETEEN: CONVERGENCE

1. I certainly do not want to belittle or minimize anyone's heartfelt plea to God—especially when that plea is earnest, but seemingly in vain. There are circumstances where we just don't hear God clearly at all. Many times these circumstances are occurring in the midst of deep personal pain, stress, or turmoil. I have experienced this many times in my own life.

   This discussion is not about hearing God's voice during hard times. This discussion is merely intended to shed light on the fact that, as a rule, God is not hiding from us. The baseline intent of the father heart of God is that we should know and walk with him. Knowing God and walking with him implies explicit knowledge of his will for our lives. Also, it is not my intent to "formulize" God's will. He is God and will not be reduced to a formula. What is outlined in this chapter are time-tested principles for discerning God's will.

2. Romans 1:20

3. A. W. Tozer, *The Knowledge of the Holy* (Harper & Row, New York, New York, 1961), p. 13.

4. Ibid, p. 15.

5. John 10:30; 8:58

6. 1 Kings 19

7. Proverbs 15:22

8. 1 Samuel 15

9. John 10:4

10. 2 Corinthians 10:5

CHAPTER TWENTY: SAIL ON

1. Sun Tzu, *The Art of War,* Part III: "Act Of Strategum," translated by Randolph McMann.

2. E. M. Bounds, *The Complete Works of E. M. Bounds on Prayer* (Baker Books, Grand Rapids, Michigan, 1990), p. 179.

3. Judges 6:12–14

4. John 10:10

5. Romans 5:1–2 (The Message)

COLOPHON

Identity Theft: Reclaiming Your Freedom in Christ
by Ken White

Cover designed by Heather Seeger, cover photograph by
Andrejs Zemdega, istockphoto.com

Book created using Adobe InDesign CS3 and designed and
edited by Kit Sublett for Whitecaps Media. Original
manuscript prepared in Microsoft Word

Main body composed in Cambria 10.5 pt. Cambria was
designed by Dutch typographer Jelle Bosma in 2004,
with Steve Matteson and Robin Nicholas

Books to help you grow

You might enjoy these other titles from Whitecaps Media

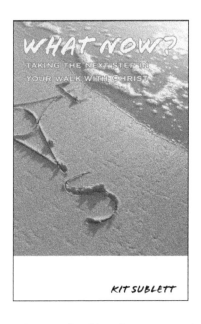

What Now? Taking the Next Step in Your Walk With Christ
by Kit Sublett
124 pages
5.5 x 8.5, paperback

This is the perfect book to give anyone who needs a simple step-by-step guide to taking their faith to the next level.
Great for groups.
Study questions available free at whitecapsmedia.com.

Find out how to order these books at whitecapsmedia.com

Wholehearted
by Roger Wernette
240 pages
5.5 x 8.5, paperback

Roger Wernette takes a fresh
look at three life-changing
commands of Jesus: learn
to love God, obey Him, and
teach others to do the same.

After the Leap by Carol Vance
264 pages
8.25 x 11, paperback

Carol Vance has taken hundreds of believers through
this course on the basics of
discipleship. This workbook
includes 25 lessons complete
with group study questions.

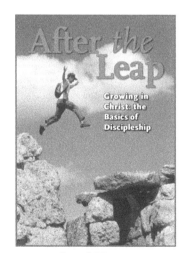

Lightning Source UK Ltd.
Milton Keynes UK
UKHW010046181121
394141UK00002B/745